MONEY, SEX, WAR, KARMA

Notes for a Buddhist Revolution

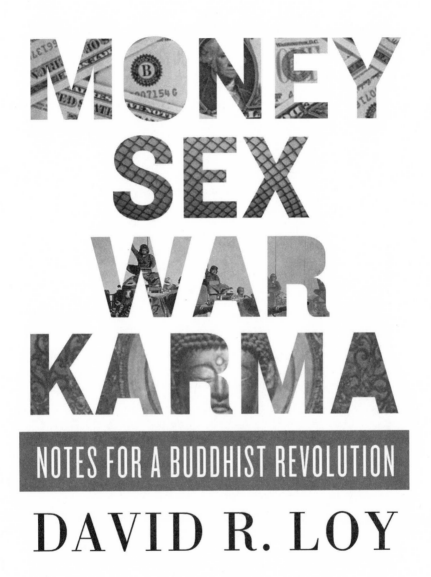

MONEY SEX WAR KARMA

NOTES FOR A BUDDHIST REVOLUTION

DAVID R. LOY

Wisdom Publications • Boston

Wisdom Publications, Inc.
199 Elm Street
Somerville MA 02144 USA
www.wisdompubs.org

Library of Congress Cataloging-in-Publication Data
Loy, David, 1947-
 Money, sex, war, karma : notes for a Buddhist revolution / David R. Loy.
   p. cm.
 Includes bibliographical references and index.
 ISBN 0-86171-558-6 (pbk. : alk. paper)
 1. Religious life—Buddhism. 2. Buddhism—Social aspects. I. Title.
 BQ5395.L69 2008
 294.3'42—dc22

                            2008002693

12 11 10
5 4 3 2

Cover design by Emily Mahon. Interior design by TL Set in Diacritical Bembo, 11.5/16.

Wisdom Publications' books are printed on acid-free paper and meet the guidelines for permanence and durability of the Production Guidelines for Book Longevity of the Council on Library Resources.

Printed in the United States of America

♻ This book was produced with environmental mindfulness. We have elected to print this title on 30% PCW recycled paper. As a result, we have saved the following resources: 10 trees, 3 million BTUs of energy, 913 lbs. of greenhouse gases, 4,398 gallons of water, and 267 lbs. of solid waste. For more information, please visit our website, www.wisdompubs.org. This paper is also FSC certified. For more information, please visit www.fscus.org..

When I look inside and see that I am nothing, that's wisdom.
When I look outside and see that I am everything, that's love.
Between these two my life turns.

—Nasargadatta Maharaj

Table of Contents

Introduction

Now that Buddhism has come to the West, how are they changing each other?

Half a century ago the British historian Arnold Toynbee predicted that their encounter would be a major event in world history. According to one account he even claimed that the arrival of Buddhism in the West "may well prove to be the most important event of the twentieth century." Given everything else that's happened in the last hundred years, one hesitates to agree with him, yet today we can appreciate better that the arrival of Buddhism does mark something special. For the first time, most of the world's major civilizations—I'm thinking of India, China, Japan, and the West—are not only interacting militarily and economically but their worldviews are in serious conversation with each other.

Nothing like this has ever happened before. Thanks to the density and speed of interaction provided by modern information and transportation technologies, the global dialogue between East and West is opening up possibilities that we cannot anticipate. This encounter also challenges Buddhism in new ways. If the Dharma is to fulfill its liberative potential, it must make the transition from being an Asian tradition (more accurately, several Asian traditions) into a teaching that speaks more directly to the spiritual needs of modern people living in a globalizing world.

What does that imply about the ways contemporary Buddhism is being taught and practiced?

Buddhism is the oldest of the world's three big missionary religions, the other two being Christianity and Islam. Each was so successful because it became the religion of an empire (in the case of Buddhism, the empire of Ashoka in the third century B.C.E., which included most of South Asia). This does not mean that Buddhism spread by the sword. Its expansion to Ceylon and Southeast Asia, and later north of the Himalayas, seems to have been a peaceful affair. In accord with its own emphasis on insubstantiality and interpenetration, Buddhism spread by infiltrating other cultures, subverting their religions to its own purposes. Native mythologies were not suppressed but *reinterpreted* in Buddhist terms. In China, for example, Mahayana Buddhism resonated with Taoism and their intercourse gave birth to Chan (Zen). In Tibet, tantric Buddhism merged with Bön shamanism and the fruit was Tibetan Buddhism.

This adaptability did not always work to Buddhism's advantage. There were many factors that led to the eventual disappearance of Buddhism in its birthplace, India, but one of them, ironically, was its influence on Brahmanism and other local traditions. Buddhism became more dispensable once some of its key elements had been absorbed. As the art historian and philosopher Ananda Coomaraswamy put it, "Brahmanism killed Buddhism with a fraternal embrace." For example, the Buddhist understanding of *nirvana* influenced Hindu notions of *moksha* liberation, and Buddhist innovations such as the two-truths doctrine were adopted and adapted by Vedanta.

This history is worth remembering as Buddhism faces its biggest transition yet. To influence the modern world, Buddhism must adapt to it. But is its present popularity another fraternal hug? The threat today is not Western religions but psychology and consumerism. Is the Dharma becoming another form of psychotherapy? Another commodity to be bought and sold? Will Western Buddhism end up all too compatible with our individualistic consumption patterns,

with expensive retreats and initiations catering to over-stressed converts eager to pursue their own enlightenment? Let's hope not,
because Buddhism and the West need each other.

Despite its economic and technological dynamism, Western civilization and its globalization are in trouble—which means all of us
are in trouble. The most obvious example is our inability to respond
to accelerating climate change as seriously as it requires, if humanity is to survive and thrive over the next few centuries. There's no
need to go on at length here about the other social and ecological
crises that confront us now, which are increasingly difficult to ignore;
many of those are considered in the following chapters. It's also
becoming harder to overlook the fact that the political and economic systems we're so proud of seem unable to address these problems. One must ask: Is that because they themselves are the problem?

Part of the problem is leadership, or the lack of it, but we can't
simply blame our rulers. It's not only the lack of a moral core among
those who rise to the top, or the institutional deformations that mas-
sage their rise. Economic and political elites (and there's not much
difference between them anymore), like the rest of us, are in need of
a new vision of human possibility: what it means to be human, why
we tend to get into trouble, and how we can get out of it. Those
who benefit most from present social arrangements may think of
themselves as hard-headed realists, but as self-conscious human
beings we remain motivated by some such vision whether we're
aware of it or not. As "Why We Love War" points out, even secular
modernity is based on a spiritual worldview—unfortunately a deficient one, from a Buddhist perspective.

The Dharma talks and essays that follow offer examples of how
Buddhist teachings can illuminate our situation. Yet influence is a
two-way street. The exotic names, robes, and rituals of Asian Buddhism
are attractive to many of us, but sooner or later we must begin to distinguish the imported forms that we appreciate from the essential

Dharma that we need. Buddhism needs to take advantage of its encounter with modern/postmodern civilization—offering a greater challenge than Buddhism has ever faced before—to engage in a self-examination that attempts to distinguish what is vital and still living in its Asian versions from what is unnecessary and perhaps outdated.

This is dangerous, of course. There is always the possibility of throwing out the baby with the bathwater—but the alternative is to keep immersing ourselves in waters that have become tepid and muddied. We should accept that the Theravada, Mahayana, and Vajrayana traditions we have learned so much from are particular historical, culturally contingent forms that the Dharma has taken in pre-modern Asia. Buddhism might have evolved differently, and today it needs to continue evolving, in order to find the ways of teaching and practices that work best for us.

I am not talking about changing the Dharma but adapting its forms, as they must always be adapted so the Dharma may thrive in a new place and time. Buddhist emphasis on impermanence (*anicca* in Pali) and insubstantiality *(anatta, shunyata)* allows and indeed obliges this adaptability. The writings of the thirteenth-century Japanese Zen master Dogen are so insightful because he challenged old metaphors that had gone stale by taking advantage of the creative possibilities of the Japanese language. Does the challenge of modernity require anything less from us? Buddhism can provide what the modern world most needs: the spiritual message that may yet awaken us to who we are and why we as a species have such a penchant for making ourselves unhappy. For that message to have its full impact, however, the Dharma must find new modes of expression that speak more directly to us, including those who may not be much interested in Asian cultures. When transplanting an exotic species into a new environment, it may be helpful to bring some of the original soil entwined with the roots. Eventually, however, the plant must become able to root itself in new ground.

The interdependence of our globalizing world implies that the evolution of Western Buddhism will also reflexively interact with Asian Buddhism. In fact, this is already happening, and that is just as well. To some extent Asian Buddhism is stuck, in much the same ways that all religious traditions tend to get stuck. The Fourteenth Dalai Lama—in many ways an inspiring example of how a religious institution can begin to change in new circumstances—has mentioned that by the time of the Chinese invasion Tibetan Buddhism had begun to fossilize, and that in some ways Tibetan Buddhism has benefited from exposure to the West. The situation of Buddhism in other Asian societies is quite different, of course, but many of the problems are similar.

As religions begin to develop so too do tensions between the founder's salvific message and the institution that arises to preserve that message. Although an organization is necessary, it's not easy to avoid a shift in focus from the original message to preserving and enhancing the status of the institution. We see this in the evolution of Buddhism as well. Shakyamuni created the Sangha as a fellowship of serious practitioners, but I wonder if he anticipated what would happen to it. Although it began as a community of wandering mendicants, thanks to many donations the Sangha eventually became quite wealthy and influential, as also happened to the medieval church in Europe.

This changed the relationship between monastics and laypeople. The Pali Canon makes it quite clear that lay men and women can also attain liberation, although they have more responsibilities and distractions to cope with. The basic challenge for them is exactly the same as for monastics: practicing the Dharma to awaken, and living a life of compassion that manifests that awakening. In much of Asian Buddhism, however, a self-defeating split has opened up between the Sangha and the laity. Today the main spiritual responsibility of lay Buddhists is not to follow the path themselves but to support *bhikkhu* monks (and, less often, *bhikkhuni* nuns). In this way lay men and women gain *punna*, "merit," which can lead to a more favorable rebirth next time, or, even better, winning the lottery this lifetime. (See "How to Drive Your Karma.")

Such spiritual materialism has had a negative effect on the Sangha too. In some cultures its main social role today is not to spread the teachings, or even to set a good example, but to serve as a "field of merit" that provides opportunities for laypeople to gain merit. According to popular belief, the more spiritually developed a bhikkhu is, the more merit a donation deposits into one's spiritual bank account. The most important thing for bhikkhus, therefore, is to follow the monastic rules and regulations (the Vinaya) strictly, and to be *seen* doing that, so that one is a worthy recipient of lay support. The result is that some Asian Sanghas and their lay supporters are locked into a co-dependent marriage where it's difficult for either partner to change.

A rather different situation exists in Japan, where many temple monks had common-law wives and children before 1872, when they became legally permitted to marry. The task of providing for them eventually transformed temples into family businesses, and the old-est son is still expected to become a priest to keep that temple business in the family, regardless of whether he has any religious inclinations. As a result, Japanese Buddhism today is, in very large part, a thriving (and lucrative) industry focused on funerals and memorial services—and not much else.

Ironically, Shakyamuni Buddha himself seems to have been quite relaxed about rules. During his lifetime many regulations were formulated to keep order among the rapidly growing monastic community, but just before he passed away the Buddha emphasized that only the major rules were important; the rest could be discarded. Unfortunately no one thought to ask him which were the major rules, so afterward the Sangha ignored his hint and decided to keep them all. We are reminded that the Buddha was more flexible and open-minded than the institutions that developed to preserve his teachings. Today we find ourselves in a situation where that flexibility needs to be recovered.

To sum up, the encounter that Toynbee had such high hopes for is between a West in crisis and a Buddhism that has its own problems. This does not diminish the importance of their interaction. Quite the opposite: it means that both sides need each other. Each has much to learn from the other as well as to offer the other. On the Buddhist side, we need to do more than translate traditional categories into modern terminology. Today some Buddhist teachings are more comprehensible to us than they could have been in the Buddha's day. The Buddhist emphasis on *anatta,* "not-self," makes more sense to modern psychologists who understand the ego-self as a mental construction. (See "The Suffering of Self.") Linguists and philosophers have caught up with Nagarjuna's realization that language constructs reality, and usually deceives us in the process. (See "The Second Buddha.") Our understanding of Buddhism can benefit from these modern developments. On the other side, some things make less sense to us today. Although we can understand better the Buddha's critique of ritual and his emphasis on motivation and intentions, we need to rethink our often inconsistent views of karma and rebirth. (See "How to Drive Your Karma.")

The essays that follow try to do more than wrap the Dharma in modern clothes. What is most illuminating is when two different ways of thinking encounter and interrogate each other sympathetically, in a mutual search for new understanding. The results have significant implications for each side. We can begin to see more clearly what is essential about the Buddha's Dharma, and we also begin to see more clearly its extraordinary implications for the situation we find ourselves in. As the Buddhist path is demythologized, its relevance today becomes more apparent.

Of course it's presumptuous to talk about "liberating Buddhism," but there's something to be said for the *double-entendre:* a more liberated Buddhism is a more liberative Buddhism. Although both concerns are present in each of the chapters that follow, "liberated Buddhism" is the main focus in the first half of this book, which offers some innovative ways of expressing the Dharma. "Liberative Buddhism" is emphasized in the second half, where the Dharma offers us fresh ways to understand the fix we're in today. In every chapter, however, it is my hope that each perspective benefits from the other.

"The Suffering of Self" goes to the heart of what is most distinctive about Buddhism: the link it reveals between our inability to enjoy life and our delusive sense of self. How are they connected, and how can the delusion of self be overcome? The sense of self is shadowed by a sense of *lack* that we feel but do not understand, so we usually try to resolve it in ways that just make things worse. Since this problem is basically spiritual—in fact it's *the* spiritual problem, at the root of many, perhaps most other, problems—the solution must also be spiritual. We need to stop evading the emptiness at our core and realize its true nature.

"Lack of Money," "The Great Seduction," and "Trapped in Time" use that perspective to understand how our ways of thinking about money, fame, and time have become delusions that "bind us without a rope." Why do we never have enough of them? The desire for money is often obsessive because money functions as a kind of symbolic reality that can fill up our sense of lack. Money as a social construct is of course valueless in itself—you can't eat or drink a dollar bill—but as our medium of exchange it is the most valuable thing of all. Inevitably, then, it has come to represent abstract happiness. Remember Midas? Today there's a bit of him in most of us. There is nothing wrong with having money if you know how to use it well, but we're in for trouble when we expect something from it that it can't provide.

Is the same true for fame? We tend to assume that fame, like money, is a universal craving, but neither of them was very important in the European middle ages. Modern fame requires modern media: television and film, newspapers and magazines, and so forth. Why has the prospect of fame become so attractive to us? To understand that we also need to consider the alternative: what Leo Braudy calls the "living death" of anonymity in a world increasingly dominated by electronic media. The collective attention of so many unknown people seems to offer us a potent way, perhaps the best way, to feel more real. Since it can't really make us more real, however, this possibility is better understood as a collective delusion.

An even more troublesome issue for many of us is time, or the lack of it. Is our lack of time also connected with our lack of self? Not only is there never enough time to do everything we want, there never *can* be enough time, because we know our time is limited and we know what is going to happen at the end of it. Buddhism doesn't promise immortality in the usual sense—living on and on, forever—but it offers a different solution to our time-stress, which involves a new understanding of time. Time isn't something I have, it's something I am, and if I *am* time then I can't be trapped *by* it. Paradoxically, to *become* time by realizing my nonduality with it—what Dogen called *uji*, "being-time"—is to live in an eternal present.

Our usual way of thinking about time, and how we get trapped "in" it, is a good example of how we make conceptual distinctions that we then get stuck in—for example, the delusive distinction between *me* and *my time*. The ancient Indian philosopher Nagarjuna, generally agreed to be the second most important figure in the history of Buddhism, wrote about such dualisms and how they deceive us. What he had to say is very important but his philosophical style is condensed and not easy to understand. "The Second Buddha" offers an overview of his teachings and how modern philosophers are finally catching up with what he realized almost two thousand years ago.

One of the most important issues for contemporary Buddhism is *karma.* How should it be understood today? As impermanence implies, karma too has a history, and that history comes with its own baggage. The most common literal interpretation implies that social justice is built into the moral fabric of the universe: someone born blind or poor is reaping the consequences of deeds in a previous life-time. Unlike *anatta,* "not-self," and many other Buddhist teachings, however, there is no modern support for such a view; science has discovered no such force or mechanism. That in itself does not refute such an interpretation but it does suggest that we should consider other explanations. The problem, again, is that karma is usually understood as something that the self *has,* rather than something that the sense of self *is.* "How to Drive Your Karma" presents this "new" perspective. For the Buddha the most important point about karma was that it's the key to spiritual development, because it reveals how our lives can be changed right here and now by changing the motivations behind what we do.

Another issue that many contemporary Buddhists are confused about is sex. Is Buddhism compatible with contemporary attitudes toward sexuality and gender? Although celibacy is not necessary for laypeople, it is required of monastics. Does that have implications for those who are not monastics but who also take their practice very seriously? Is it better for our spiritual development if the rest of us are celibate too? "What's Wrong with Sex?" tries to answer that question by considering why celibacy has been so important for Buddhist monastics. Just as important, we need to think about what we today expect from romance and sex, especially our continual hope that they can somehow fill up our sense of lack.

Our world is quite different from the Buddha's. If he were living today, what would the Buddha do? That question is not easy to answer yet it's not one that we can ignore either. The globalization of economic, military, and ecological crises gives new meaning to the Buddhist emphasis on interdependence, and calls for new types of bodhisattvas—for all of us to respond as best we can. But if everything is "empty," what's the urgency? In order to really help the world, shouldn't we focus on our own awakening first? Or do those objections misunderstand the Buddhist path? "What Would the Buddha Do?" takes up these questions.

"The Three Poisons, Institutionalized" reflects further on what distinguishes our situation from that of the Buddha. He emphasized the importance of transforming the three unwholesome motivations: greed into generosity, ill will into loving-kindness, delusion into wisdom. Today we also have to address their collective versions: our economic system institutionalizes greed, militarism institutionalizes ill will, and the media institutionalize delusion. Any personal awakening we might have on our cushions remains incomplete until it is supplemented by a "social awakening" and a social response to these institutionalized causes of widespread suffering.

Buddhist awakening liberates our awareness from grasping fixations. As well as institutionalized greed, ill will, and delusion, today we are subjected to new types of *attention traps* that are discussed in "Consciousness Commodified." Our awareness is conditioned in new ways: fragmented by new information and communication technologies, commodified by advertising and consumerism, and manipulated by sophisticated propaganda techniques. Who owns our collective attention, and who has the right to decide what happens to it?

Although you wouldn't know it from the news media, no problem today is more important than global climate change and related ecological crises that threaten the continuation of civilization as we know it. Why are we so incapable of responding to these challenges with the seriousness they deserve? "Healing Ecology" offers a Buddhist perspective based upon the delusion of self and the lack that haunts it. If my fundamental personal problem is the delusion of separation from others, is that also true collectively? If the parallel holds, our alienation from the rest of the biosphere must be an ongoing source of collective anxiety for us, and our attempts to secure ourselves are just making things worse. Why is our GNP never big enough? Why do we never have enough technology?

"The Karma of Food" offers an example of how a Buddhist perspective might help us evaluate new technologies, specifically the benefits and dangers of genetically modified (GM) food. Although at least one Buddhist organization has condemned GM food as unnatural, there is little concern for "being natural" in traditional Buddhist teachings. A better way to address this issue is to remember Buddhist emphasis on the karmic consequences of motivation. How much are food corporations focusing on what is beneficial for consumers and the biosphere, and how much are they motivated by institutionalized greed and delusion?

"Why We Love War" reflects on the unfortunate paradox that, although everyone professes to hate war, we keep doing it. Is that because war is yet another way of trying to resolve our sense of lack? Do we have to fight against the bad guys *over there* in order to feel good about who we are *here*? Historically, the attempt to get rid of evil people has usually ended up creating more evil. Isn't that also true of the War on Terror? If terrorism is the war of the poor, war is the terrorism of the rich. Perhaps we can't understand the enduring attraction of war or terrorism until we understand the festering sense of lack built into secular modernity, which seems to offer us different ways to become happy but can't explain why they don't actually make us happy.

It's relatively easy to see the problems. How can Buddhism help us solve them? "Notes for a Buddhist Revolution" argues that socially engaged Buddhism does not imply a distinctive social movement. Along with other engaged spiritualities, however, it may have an important role to play in what has become a global movement for peace and social justice. Buddhism contributes an emphasis on personal spiritual practice, commitment to non-violence, the flexibility implied by impermanence and nonsubstantiality *(anatta* and *shunyata),* along with the realization that ending our own *dukkha* requires us to address the *dukkha* of everyone else as well.

These have many implications for how we engage, but what should socially engaged Buddhists focus on? While we certainly need to address the militarization of our society and the ecological impact of our economy, Buddhist emphasis on the liberation of awareness suggests a more distinctive critique of the ways that our collective awareness has become trapped and manipulated. Does that also imply where we should focus our efforts?

The Suffering of Self

If someone asked you to summarize the teachings of the Buddha, what would you say? For most Buddhists, probably the first thing that would come to mind is the four noble (or "ennobling") truths: *dukkha,* its causes, its cessation (better known as *nirvana*), and the eight-fold path that leads to cessation. Shakyamuni Buddha himself is believed to have emphasized those four truths in his first Dharma talk, and those of us who teach Buddhism find them quite helpful, because all his other teachings can be included somewhere within them.

Nevertheless, there is nothing exclusively or distinctively Buddhist about any of the four noble truths.

Buddhism has its own take on them, of course, but in their basic form the four noble truths are common to many Indian religious traditions. *Dukkha* is where most of those spiritual paths begin, including Jainism and Sankhya-Yoga. There is also wide agreement that the cause of *dukkha* is craving, and that liberation from craving is possible. Moreover, they all include some sort of way to realize that liberation. Yoga, for example, teaches a path with eight limbs that is quite similar to Buddhism's eightfold path.

So what is truly distinctive about the Buddhist Dharma? How does it differ from other religious traditions that also explain the world and our role within it? No other spiritual path focuses so clearly on the intrinsic connection between *dukkha* and our delusive sense of self. They are not only related: for Buddhism the self *is dukkha.*

Although *dukkha* is usually translated as "suffering," that is too narrow. The point of *dukkha* is that even those who are wealthy and healthy experience a basic dissatisfaction, a dis-ease, which continually festers. That we find life dissatisfactory, one damn problem after another, is not accidental—because it is the very nature of an unawakened sense-of-self to be bothered about something.

Early Buddhism distinguishes three basic types of *dukkha*. Everything we usually identify as physical and mental suffering—including being separated from those we want to be with, and being stuck with those we don't want to be with (the Buddha had a sense of humor!)—is included in the first type.

The second type is the *dukkha* due to impermanence. It's the realization that, although I might be enjoying an ice-cream cone right now, it will soon be finished. The best example of this type is awareness of mortality, which haunts our appreciation of life. Knowing that death is inevitable casts a shadow that usually hinders our ability to live fully now.

The third type of dukkha is more difficult to understand because it's connected with the delusion of self. It is dukkha due to *sankhara,* "conditioned states," which is sometimes taken as a reference to the ripening of past karma. More generally, however, *sankhara* refers to the constructedness of all our experience, including the experience of self. When looked at from the other side, another term for this constructedness is *anatta,* "not-self." There is no unconditioned self within our constructed sense of self, and this is the source of the deepest *dukkha,* our worst anguish.

This sense of being a self that is separate from the world I am in is illusory—in fact, it is our most dangerous delusion. Here we can benefit from what has become a truism in contemporary psychology, which has also realized that the sense of self is a psychological-social-linguistic construct: *psychological,* because the ego-self is a product of mental conditioning; *social,* because a sense of self develops in relation with other constructed selves; and *linguistic,* because acquiring a sense of self involves learning to use certain names and pronouns such as *I, me, mine, myself,* which create the illusion that there must be some *thing* being referred to. If the word *cup* refers to this thing I'm drinking coffee out of, then we mistakenly infer that *I* must refer to something in the same way. This is one of the ways language misleads us.

Despite these similarities to modern psychology, however, Buddhism differs from most of it in two important ways. First, Buddhism emphasizes that there is always something uncomfortable about our constructed sense of self. Much of contemporary psychotherapy is concerned with helping us become "well-adjusted." The ego-self needs to be repaired so it can fit into society and we can play our social roles better. Buddhism isn't about helping us become well-adjusted. A socially well-adjusted ego-self is still a sick ego-self, for there remains something problematical about it. It is still infected by *dukkha.*

This suggests the other way that Buddhism differs from modern psychology. Buddhism agrees that the sense of self can be reconstructed, and that it needs to be reconstructed, but it emphasizes even more that the sense of self needs to be *deconstructed,* to realize its true "empty," non-dwelling nature. Awakening to our constructedness is the only real solution to our most fundamental anxiety. Ironically, the problem and its solution both depend upon the same fact: a constructed *sense* of self is not a real self. Not being a real self is intrinsically uncomfortable. Not being a real self is also what enables the sense of self to be deconstructed and reconstructed, and this deconstruction/reconstruction is what the Buddhist spiritual path is about.

Why is a constructed sense of self so uncomfortable? "My" sense of self is composed of mostly habitual ways of perceiving, feeling, thinking, and acting. That's all. Those impermanent processes interact with others and give rise to a sense of being a self that is separate from other people and things. If you strip away those psychological and physical processes, it's like peeling off the layers of an onion. When you get to the end, what's left? Nothing. There's no hard seed or anything else at the core, once the last few layers have been peeled away. And what's wrong with that? *Nothing.* The basic problem is, we don't like being nothing. A gaping hole at one's core is quite distressing. Nothing means there's no-thing to identify with or cling to. Another way to say it is that my nothing-ness means my constructed sense of self is ungrounded, so it is haunted by a basic sense of unreality and insecurity. A sense of self can never become secure because it is nothing that could be secure.

Our English word *person* comes from the Latin *persona,* "mask." The sense of self is a mask. Who is wearing the mask? Behind the mask (form) is nothing (emptiness). That there is nothing behind the mask is not actually a problem—but unfortunately the persona does not usually know this.

(Don't be misled by these metaphors: peeling off onion layers to reach the *core,* or looking for what's *behind* the mask. In fact, that way of thinking is part of the problem: we usually make a deluded distinction between ourselves *inside* and the rest of the world *outside.*)

Intellectually, this situation is not easy to understand, but I suspect that most of us actually have some innate awareness of the problem. In fact, if our sense of self is truly empty in this way, we *must* have some basic awareness of this problem—yet it's a very uncomfortable awareness, because we don't understand it or know what to do about it. I think this is one of the great secrets of life: each of us individually experiences this sense of unreality as the feeling that "something is wrong with me." Growing up is learning to pretend along with everyone else that "I'm okay; you're okay." A lot of social interaction is about reassuring each other and ourselves that we're all really okay even though inside we feel somehow that we're not. When we look at other people from the outside, they seem quite solid and real to us, yet each of us feels deep inside that something is not right—something is wrong at the core.

Here another modern psychological idea is helpful: repression. Although Freud's legacy has become quite controversial, his concept of repression, and "the return of the repressed," remains very important. Repression happens when I become aware of something uncomfortable that I don't want to deal with, so it is "pushed away" from consciousness. Freud believed that our main repression is sexual desires. Existential psychology shifts the focus to death: our inability to cope with mortality, the fact that our lives will come to an end, and we don't know when—maybe soon. For Buddhism, however, fear of death focuses on what will happen in the future, while there is a more basic problem that we experience right *now*: this uncomfortable sense of unreality at our core, which we don't know how to deal with. Naturally enough, we learn to ignore or repress it, but that doesn't resolve the problem. The difficulty with repression is that it doesn't work. What has been repressed returns to consciousness one way or another, in a disguised or distorted fashion. This "return of the repressed" is thus a *symptom* of the original awareness that we didn't want to deal with.

Our repressed sense of unreality returns to consciousness as the feeling that there is something missing or lacking in my life. What is it that's lacking? How I understand that depends upon the kind of person I am and the kind of society I live in. The sense that *something* is wrong with me is too vague, too amorphous. It needs to be given more specific form if I'm to be able to do something about it, and that form usually depends upon how I've been raised. In modern developed (or "economized") societies such as the United States, I am likely to understand my lack as not having enough money—regardless of how much money I already have. Money is important to us not only because we can buy anything with it, but also because it has become a kind of collective *reality symbol*. The more money you get, the more real you become! That's the way we tend to think, anyway. (When a wealthy person arrives somewhere his or her presence is acknowledged much more than the arrival of a "nobody.") Because money doesn't really end *dukkha*—it can't fill up the bottomless hole at one's core—this way of thinking often becomes a trap. You're a multi-millionaire but still feel like something is wrong with your life? Obviously you don't have enough money yet.

Another example is fame. If I am known by lots and lots of people, then I must be real, right? Yet the attention of other people, who are haunted by their own sense of lack, can't fill up our sense of lack. If you think that fame is what will make you real, you can never be famous enough. The same is true of power. We crave power because it is a visible expression of one's reality. Dictators like Hitler and Stalin dominate their societies. As their biographies reveal, however, they never seem to have enough control to feel really secure. Those who want power the most end up the most paranoid.

This understanding of *anatta* gives us some insight into karma, especially the Buddha's take on it, which emphasized the role of motivations and intentions. If my sense of self is actually composed of habitual ways of perceiving, feeling, thinking, and behaving, then karma isn't something I have, it's what I *am*. The important point is that I change my karma by changing who "I" am: by reconstructing my habitual ways of perceiving, feeling, thinking, and behaving. The problematical motivations that cause so much trouble for myself and for others—greed, ill will, and delusion, the three unwholesome roots—need to be transformed into their more positive counterparts that work to reduce *dukkha:* generosity, loving-kindness, and wisdom.

Whether or not you believe in karma as something magical, as an objective moral law of the universe, on a more psychological level karma is about how habitual ways of thinking and acting tend to create predictable types of situations. If I'm motivated by greed, ill will, and delusion, then I need to be manipulative, which alienates other people and also makes me feel more separate from them. Ironically, I'm busy trying to defend and promote the interests of something that doesn't exist: my self. (And because the sense of self is not a real self, it's always in need of defense and support.) Yet acting in that way reinforces my delusive sense of self. When I'm motivated by generosity and loving-kindness, however, I can relax and open up, be less defensive. Again, other people tend to respond in the same way, which works to reduce *dukkha* for all of us.

Transforming our karma in this way is very important, yet it is not the only goal of Buddhist practice. Fundamentally, Buddhism is about awakening, which means realizing something about the constructedness of the sense of self and the nothing at its core. If changing karma involves *re*constructing the sense of self, *de*constructing the sense of self involves directly experiencing its emptiness. Usually that void at our core is so uncomfortable that we try to evade it, by identifying with something else that might give us stability and security. Another way to say it is that we keep trying to fill up that hole, yet it's a bottomless pit. Nothing that we can ever grasp or achieve can end our sense of lack.

So what happens when we don't run away from that hole at our core? That's what we're doing when we meditate: we are "letting go" of all the physical and mental activity that distracts us from our emptiness. Instead, we just sit with it and as it. It's not that easy to do, because the hole gives us such a feeling of insecurity, ungroundedness, unreality. Meditation is uncomfortable, especially at the beginning, because in our daily lives we are used to taking evasive action. So we tend to take evasive action when we meditate too: we fantasize, make plans, feel sorry for ourselves...

But if I can learn to not run away, to stay with those uncomfortable feelings, to become friendly with them, then something can happen to that core—and to me, insofar as that hole is what "I" really am. The curious thing about my emptiness is that it is not really a problem. The problem is that we think it's a problem. Our ways of trying to escape it make it into a problem.

Some Buddhist sutras talk about *paravritti,* a "turning around" that transforms the festering hole at my core into a life-healing flow which springs up spontaneously from I-know-not-where. Instead of being experienced as a sense of lack, the empty core becomes a place where there is now awareness of something other than, more than, my usual sense of self. I can never grasp that "more than," I can never understand what it is—and I do not need to, because "I" am an expression of it. My role is to become a better manifestation of it, with less interference from the delusion of ego-self. So our emptiness has two sides: the negative, problematic aspect is a sense of lack. The other aspect is being in touch with, and manifesting, something greater than my sense of self—that is, something more than I usually understand myself to be. The original Buddhist term usually translated as emptiness (Pali *shunnata;* Sanskrit *shunyata*) actually has this double-sided meaning. It derives from the root *shu,* which means "swollen" in both senses: not only the swollenness of a blown-up balloon but also the swollenness of an expectant woman, pregnant with possibility. So a more accurate translation of *shunyata* would be: emptiness/fullness, which describes quite well the experience of our own empty core, both the problem and the solution.

These two ways of experiencing our emptiness are not mutually exclusive. I think many of us go back and forth, often bothered by our sense of lack, but also occasionally experiencing our emptiness more positively as a source of spontaneity and creativity, like athletes do when they are "in the zone." The point isn't to get rid of the self: that's not possible, for there never has been a self. Nor do we want to get rid of the *sense* of self: that would be a rather unpleasant type of mental retardation. Rather, what we work toward is a more permeable, less dualistic sense of self, which is more aware of, and more comfortable with, its empty constructedness.

The two aspects of the spiritual path, deconstructing and reconstructing one's sense of self, reinforce each other. Meditation is letting-go, getting back to the emptiness/fullness at our core, and this practice also helps to reconstruct the sense of self, most obviously by helping us become more mindful in daily life. Each process assists the other indefinitely. As the Japanese proverb says, even the Buddha is only halfway there. Buddhist practice is about dwelling in our empty core, which also reconstructs us into less *self*-ish, more compassionate beings devoted to the welfare and awakening of everyone.

Lack of Money

hat is money? Can Buddhism help us understand it? These seem like silly questions. After all, we use money every day, so we must have some basic understanding of what it is…but is that really so? Perhaps our familiarity with it has the opposite effect, keeping us from appreciating just how unique and strange money actually is.

Take out a dollar bill and look at it. What do you have in your hands? A piece of paper, obviously. You can't eat it, ride in it, or sleep on it. It can't shelter you when it rains, or warm you when you're cold, or heal you when you're ill, or comfort you when you're lonely. You could burn it, but an old newspaper would be much more useful if you want to start a fire. In itself that dollar bill is less useful than a blank sheet of paper, which at least we could use to write on. In and of itself, it is literally worthless, a *nothing*.

Yet money is also the most valuable thing in the world, simply because we have collectively agreed to make it so. Money is a social construction that we tend to forget is only a construct—a kind of group fantasy. The anthropologist Weston LaBarre called it a psychosis that has become normal, "an institutionalized dream that everyone is having at once." As long as we keep dreaming together it continues to work as the socially agreed-upon *means* that enables us to convert something (for example, a day's work) into something else (a couple bags of groceries, perhaps).

But, as we know, money always has the potential to turn into a curse. In addition to the usual social problems—in particular, the growing gap between those who have too much and those who have too little—there is a more basic issue. The temptation with money is to sacrifice everything else (the earth becomes "resources," our time becomes "labor," our relationships become "contacts" to be exploited, etc.) for that "pure means." To some degree that's necessary, of course. Like it or not, we live in a monetized world. The danger is that psychologically we will reverse means and ends, so that the means of life becomes the goal itself. As Arthur Schopenhauer put it, money is abstract happiness, so someone who is no longer capable of concrete happiness sets his whole heart on money. Money ends up becoming "frozen desire"—not desire for anything in particular, but a symbol for desire in general. And what does the second noble (or "ennobling") truth identify as the cause of *dukkha*?

The Greek myth of Midas and his golden touch gives us the classic metaphor for what happens when money becomes an end in itself. Midas was a Lydian king who was offered any reward he wanted for helping the god Dionysus. Although already fabulously wealthy, his greed was unsatisfied and he asked that whatever he touched might turn to gold. Midas enjoyed transforming everything into gold—until it was dinnertime. He took a bite—*ching!* It turned to gold. He took a sip of wine—*ching!* He hugged his daughter— *ching!* She turned into a golden statue. In despair, Midas asked Dionysus to deliver him from this curse, and fortunately for him the god was kind enough to oblige.

Today this simple yet profound story is even more relevant than it was in ancient Greece, because the world we live in is so much more monetized. Nowadays Midas is socially acceptable—in fact, perhaps there is a bit of Midas in all of us. Living in a world that emphasizes instant convertibility tends to de-emphasize our senses and dull our awareness of them, in favor of the magical numbers that appear and disappear in bank accounts. Instead of appreciating fully the sensuous qualities of a glass of wine, often we are more aware of how much it cost and what that implies about us as sophisticated wine-drinkers. Because we live in a society which values those magical numbers as the most important thing of all, most of us are anxious about having enough money, and often enough that anxiety is appropriate. But what is enough, and when does financial planning become the pursuit of abstract happiness? Focusing on an abstraction that has no value in itself, we depreciate our concrete, sensuous life in the world. We end up knowing the price of everything and the value of nothing. Can Buddhism help us understand why such traps are so alluring?

Today money serves at least four functions for us. For better and worse, it is indispensable as our *medium of exchange*. In effect, as I've said, this makes money more valuable than anything else, since it can transform into almost anything. What's more, because of how our society has agreed to define value, money has come to symbolize *pure value.*

Inevitably, then, money as a medium of exchange evolved into a second function. It is our *storehouse of value*. Centuries ago, before money became widely used, one's wealth was measured in cows, full granaries, servants, and children. The advantage of gold and silver—and now bank accounts—is that they are incorruptible, at least in principle, and invulnerable to rats, fire, and disease. Our fascination with gold has much to do with the fact that, unlike silver, it doesn't even tarnish. It is, in effect, immortal. This is quite attractive in a world haunted by impermanence and death.

Capitalism added another little twist, which brings us to the third function of money. It's something we take for granted today but which was suspicious, not to say immoral, to many people in the past. Capitalism is based on *capital,* which is *money used to make more money*. Invest your surplus and watch it grow! This encouraged an economic dynamism and growth that we tend to take for granted today yet is really quite extraordinary. It has led to many developments that have been beneficial but there is also a downside, when you keep re-investing whatever you get to get even more, on the assumption that you can never have *too much.* Capital can always be used to accumulate more capital. Psychologically, of course, this tends to become the much more insidious problem that you can never have *enough.* This attitude toward money is in striking contrast with the way that some premodern societies would redistribute wealth when it reached a certain level—for example, the potlatch of native communities in British Columbia. Such societies seem to have been more sensitive to the ways wealth-accumulation tends to disrupt social relationships.

The other side of capital investment is debt. A capitalist economy is an economy that runs on debt and requires a society that is comfortable with indebtedness. The debt is at least a little larger than the original loan: those who invest expect to get more back than their original investment. When this is how the whole economy works, the social result is a generalized pressure for continuous growth and expansion, because that is the only way to repay the accumulating debt. This constant pressure for growth is indifferent to other social and ecological consequences. The result is a collective future orientation: the present is never enough but the future will be (or *must* be) better.

Why do we fall into such obsessions? The *anatta* "not-self" teaching gives Buddhism a special perspective on our *dukkha,* which also implies a special take on our hang-ups with money. The problem isn't just that I will someday get sick, grow old, and die. My lack of self means that I feel something is wrong with me right now. I experience the hole at the core of my being as a sense of lack, and in response I become preoccupied with projects that I believe can make me feel more "real." Christianity has an explanation for this lack and offers a religious solution, but many of us don't believe in sin anymore. So what is wrong with us? The most popular explanation in developed or "economized" societies is that we don't have enough money. That's our contemporary "original sin."

This points to the fourth function of money for us. Beyond its usefulness as a medium of exchange and a storehouse of value and capital for investment, money has become our most important *reality symbol.* Today money is generally believed to be the best way to secure oneself/one's self, to gain a sense of solid identity, to cope with the gnawing intuition that we do not really exist. Suspecting that the sense of self is groundless, we used to visit temples and churches to ground ourselves in a relationship with God or gods. Now we invest in "securities" and "trust funds" to ground ourselves economically. Financial institutions have become our shrines.

Needless to say, there is a karmic rebound. The more we value money, the more we find it used—and the more we use it ourselves—to evaluate *us.* Money takes on a life of its own, and we end up being manipulated by the symbol we take so seriously. In this sense, the problem is not that we are too materialistic but that we are *not materialistic enough,* because we are so preoccupied with the *symbolism* that we end up devaluing life itself. We are infatuated less with the things that money can buy than with their power and status—not so much with the comfort and power of an expensive car as with what owning a Mercedes-Benz says about *me.* "I am the kind of guy who drives a Mercedes / owns a condo on Maui / and has a stock portfolio worth a million bucks…"

All this is a classic example of "binding ourselves without a rope," to use the Zen metaphor. We become trapped by our ways of thinking about money.

The basic difficulty, from a Buddhist perspective, is that we are trying to resolve a spiritual problem—our "emptiness"—by identifying with something outside ourselves, which can never confer the sense of reality we crave. We work hard to acquire a big bank account and all the things that society teaches us will make us happy, and then we cannot understand why they do not make us happy, why they do not resolve our sense that something is lacking. Is the reason really that we don't have enough *yet?*

I think that Buddhism gives us the best metaphor to understand money: *shunyata,* the "emptiness" that characterizes all phenomena. The Buddhist philosopher Nagarjuna warns us not to grab this snake by the wrong end, because there is no such thing as *shunyata.* It is a shorthand way to describe the interdependence of things, how nothing self-exists because everything is part of everything else. If we misunderstand the concept and cling to *shunyata,* the cure becomes worse than the disease. Money—also nothing in itself, nothing more than a socially agreed-upon symbol—remains indispensable today. But woe to those who grab this snake by the tail. As the *Heart Sutra* teaches, all form is empty, yet there is no emptiness apart from form. Preoccupation with money is fixation on something that has no meaning in itself, apart from the forms it takes, forms that we become less and less able to truly appreciate.

Another way to make this point is that money is not a *thing* but a *process.* Perhaps it's best understood as an energy that is not really mine or yours. Those who understand that it is an empty, socially-constructed symbol can use it wisely and compassionately to reduce the world's suffering. Those who use it to become more real end up being used by it, their alienated sense of self clutching a blank check—a promissory note that can never be cashed.

The Great Seduction

Why would anyone in his right mind want to become famous—I mean *really* famous? I know that fame is often convertible into other things that we crave: money (selling your story to the newspapers), sexual attraction (people throwing themselves at your feet), power (fame is roughly equivalent to success for actors and politicians). But what's enjoyable about being so well-known that you can't walk down a sidewalk without the risk of being mobbed?

You might enjoy such attention the first time, yet the need to protect yourself would soon make it burdensome, and sometimes dangerous. The nuisance of stalkers points to a bigger problem. Not everyone will be satisfied to admire you from afar. You can't simply turn off your celebrity when it is inconvenient, because it doesn't belong to you. You are the center of a network that involves other people. Your appearance, words, and actions are publicly available and scrutinized. Famous people can't help getting caught up in our fantasies about who they (and we) are. People relate not to you but to what you mean for them. Remember what happened to John Lennon?

Lennon's kind of fame is a relatively recent development. It requires modern media such as newspapers, magazines, and television. Word of mouth isn't enough. Of course, from the very beginning of civilization there have always been some famous people, usually rulers and conquerors. Kings had bards to compose songs celebrating their achievements. In those days that was the only way to record one's exploits for posterity. There were also religious teachers such as Jesus and the Buddha. One of the most famous figures in pre-modern Europe was Saint Francis of Assisi. He was renowned because of his sanctity—that is, his close relationship with God. His fame was a side-effect of what he was believed to be.

We can wonder about whether fame was a burden for Saint Francis, but what was life like for all those other people during his time who were not famous, and who maybe never saw anyone who was? Today we tend to suppose that everyone longs for personal fame, yet according to historians medieval people had no such desire. Our assumption reveals more about us than about them, which encourages us to reflect: why has the prospect of fame become so seductive to us? Why are so many people eager to make fools of themselves on *Big Brother*? And why are so many other people keen to watch them?

New technologies offer new possibilities. It's no coincidence that the modern world began roughly the same time as the printing press. Print offered not only a new medium for fame but also a new kind of fame: the bestselling author. As with Saint Francis, Shakespeare's reputation was a side-effect of something else—in his case, an unparalleled literary imagination. Today, in contrast, we have *celebrities:* people who are famous mainly for being famous, since most of us have forgotten how they became famous. No one questions this because fame is now accepted as an end in itself. Celebrities continue to be celebrated because the media need them as much as they need the media. Television, like politics, thrives not on stories or ideas but on personalities.

In the last century the number of famous people has rapidly proliferated because everyday life has become so much more dominated by the media. We spend increasingly large portions of our time plugged into one or another of the electronic media, which now function as our collective nervous system. At the same time, desire for fame has become so ubiquitous that we no longer notice it, any more than fish see the water they swim in. It has infiltrated all the corners of our culture, including Christmas carols ("Then how the reindeer loved him/ As they shouted out in glee,/ 'Rudolf the red-nosed reindeer/ You'll go down in history!'") and spaghetti sauce bottles (see the label on Newman's Own Spaghetti Sauce).

What does this fascination with celebrity mean for those of us who aren't famous? How has it affected our own self-image? Instead of taking this collective obsession for granted, we'd do better to ask where it comes from. We can't make sense of it, I think, unless we consider the alternative. We don't understand the attraction of fame until we realize what is unattractive about being not-famous. In a culture so permeated by print and electronic images, where the media now determine what is real and what is not, being anonymous amounts to being no one at all. To be unknown is to feel like we are nothing, for our lack of being is constantly contrasted with all those *real* people whose images dominate the screen, and whose names keep appearing in the newspapers and magazines. In his book *The Frenzy of Renown,* Leo Braudy sums it up well: "the essential lure of the famous is that they are somehow more real than we are and that our insubstantial physical reality needs that immortal substance for support…because it is the best, perhaps the only, way *to be.*"

If self-justifying fame is the way to become more real, then one way to become real is to be really bad. "How many times do I have to kill before I get a name in the paper or some national attention?" wrote a serial killer to the Wichita police. Only with his sixth murder, he complained, had he begun to get the publicity he deserved. More recently, the Virginia Tech gunman Seung-Hui Cho succeeded in making himself into someone who will not soon be forgotten. According to Braudy such fame "promises acceptability, even if one commits the most heinous crime, because thereby people will finally know who you are, and you will be saved from the living death of being unknown."

People in low-tech medieval times had their own problems, but *the living death of being unknown* was not one of them. Since fame was so rare and not really a possibility for anyone except a few rulers, anonymity was not the curse for them that it has become for us. It was not their solution to lack.

"How can he be dead, who lives immortal in the hearts of men?" mused Longfellow about Michelangelo. Freud defined immortality as "being loved by many anonymous people," yet our desire for that kind of impersonal love reveals just as much about our craving for fame right here and now. What makes that person on the screen seem more *real* to us, if not that we're all looking at her?

The basic problem is that preoccupation with fame plugs all too easily into the sense of *lack* that haunts our sense of self. That it's a construct means the sense of self is always ungrounded and insecure. That it's a product of psychological and social conditioning means that it develops in response to the attention of others, especially parents, siblings, and friends. Even as adults, therefore, we quite naturally try to reassure ourselves with the approbation of other people. Much of the value of money for us is due to its supposed effects on the opinion of others. As much as Donald Trump may enjoy his wealth, he obviously craves public admiration as much, if not more.

One difference between medieval people and us is that they believed in a different kind of salvation. If they lived as God wanted them to, He would take care of them. Today fewer people believe in God or an afterlife, which makes us more susceptible to secular solutions that promise to fill up our sense of lack right here.

The irony of a celebrity-obsessed culture is that, whether you're famous or a nobody, you are equally trapped if fame is important to you—that is, if fame is your way to become more real. The duality between fame and anonymity is another version of the dualistic thinking that Buddhism cautions us about. We distinguish between them because we want one rather than the other, but we can't have one without the other because they are interdependent. The meaning of each depends upon the other, since each is the opposite of the other. If I want to live a "pure" live (however that is understood), I need to keep avoiding impurity. In the same way, to the extent that I desire to be famous then I am equally worried about not being famous.

It makes no difference whether I actually *am* famous. In either case, I'm trapped in the same dualistic way of thinking. If I'm not famous, I will worry about remaining that way. If I am famous, I will also worry about remaining that way—that is, about losing my fame. Although the media need celebrities they are readily replaced. Even if my celebrity continues, I can never be famous *enough*—because no one can ever be famous enough, any more than one can ever be rich enough or thin enough. When fame symbolizes becoming more real, disappointment or disillusionment is inevitable. No amount of fame can ever satisfy if it's really something else that I am seeking from it, which it cannot provide.

As Lewis Lapham put it, "Because the public image comes to stand as the only valid certification of being, the celebrity clings to his image as the rich man clings to his money—that is, as if to life itself." But some rich people do not cling to their money. The issue, again, is whether we use money or it uses us. If we understand what money is—a social construction that is valueless in and of itself—we need not be ensnared by it. Is the same true for fame?

Unless you are very rich indeed, money can still leave you anonymous and relatively invisible, whereas fame does not. Otherwise, however, the parallel still holds. If you realize that fame, like money, cannot make you more real, you can escape the trap of trying to use it to become someone special.

For an example, consider the situation of the Dalai Lama. He has received the Nobel Peace Prize, perhaps humanity's highest honor, and he needs bodyguards (mainly because of his difficult position as an exiled head of state). Nevertheless, the Dalai Lama serves as an admirable example of how fame, like money, can be valuable when employed as a skillful means. He is such a fine Dharma teacher because he has evidently not been personally affected by his reputation as Buddhism's foremost Dharma teacher.

Trapped in Time

A lot of our *dukkha* has to do with time. We feel trapped by it. More precisely, we feel trapped *in* it. Occasionally we don't know what to do with ourselves on a rainy Sunday afternoon, but more often we can't find the time to do everything that needs to be done, or all the things we want to do. Although we'd like to be able to slow down and enjoy the moment, right here and now, there's just too much that's waiting to be done. Maybe tomorrow, or next week.

But there's a more sinister problem with time. The fact that we never seem to have enough of it points to a bigger predicament, that we *can't* ever have enough of it. What time we have will sooner or later come to an end, and that may be sooner if we're not careful—and maybe even if we are. Like everything else that lives, we're born at a certain time and pass away sometime later, yet something in us screams in denial: *No!* Not only do we want to keep living forever, we feel as if we *should* live forever. Being self-conscious means being a self conscious of its inevitable fate. How lucky unselfconscious animals are: when it's time for them to die they die, but they don't seem to spend their whole lives worrying about it.

Many religions provide an escape from death and time that distinguishes body from soul. The body dies but the soul lives on. Buddhism, however, offers a more paradoxical solution. Time and eternity are not incompatible. In fact they are like two sides of the same coin. The eternal life we desire is something we already experience right now. We just need to realize the true nature of time. In order to do that, however, we also have to realize our own true nature—because the true nature of each is not separate from the true nature of the other.

Buddhism distinguishes two truths, the relative (conventional) truth and the ultimate (absolute) truth. Since samsara, the world of suffering, is not different from nirvana, the relative truth does not refer to a different reality than the ultimate truth does. The relative truth is the way we usually experience the world, as a collection of separate things—including *us*—that arise and pass away. This occurs in time that is experienced as objective and external. The ultimate truth is realizing the way things really are, that they are not separate from each other and therefore are not really *things* in the usual sense. What does that imply about the time they are supposed to be *in*?

According to the relative truth you and I are also in time, and since we were born we will someday die; that is our *dukkha*. Death is the opposite of life, the end of life. According to the ultimate truth, however, we do not escape death because we have immortal souls. Rather, you and I cannot die; we were *never born*. That is the sense in which we are literally im-mortal, not subject to death. That is what *anatta*, "not-self," means. The sense of duality usually experienced between myself *inside* and the rest of the world *outside* is a delusion.

One way to dispel that delusion is to look for the "I" that is supposed to be inside. Hui-k'o complained to Bodhidharma that he had no peace of mind. "Show me your mind," Bodhidharma replied, "and I will pacify it for you." "I can't find it," said Hui-k'o. Bodhidharma: "Then I have pacified it for you." Recognizing there is no such mind to be grasped, that no such self can be found—that is true peace of mind. I cannot be trapped *in* time if there is no "I," and never was.

What does this mean for the ways we experience time right here and now, moment by moment? If my watch tells me it's now 7:30 P.M., how can I *at the same time* be living in eternity?

Part of the problem is that we have the wrong idea about what *eternity* means. The Argentine writer Jorge Luis Borges wrote a short story called "The Immortal," about a man who achieves immortality and then suffers from it. In the first half of the story he searches for the spring whose water grants eternal life. In the second half he searches ceaselessly for the water of another spring that would grant him death. Is eternity in the way we usually understand it—an immortality that just goes on and on forever—what we really want? Wouldn't life eventually become a burden that we would want to get rid of?

As much as we may chafe at the limited time we have, we are dependent upon those limitations. Could we play a football game without a touchdown line and out-of-bounds? If my time never came to an end then the meaning of my life would also balloon until I had no reason to do anything right now, especially anything effortful. Want to play the piano? Speak Chinese? When there's no time restriction you can do or learn anything you want—but then what would motivate you to get started today, knowing that there's never any need to hurry…and that would be just as true tomorrow, and next year, and the next century. What's the rush? Perhaps I shouldn't generalize for everyone but I'm pretty sure that I would become even lazier. Nor would it help if I decided to be hedonistic. I like chocolate a lot, but a life devoted to eating it wouldn't be fun for long. That's also true for the other pleasures I can think of. A couple days, maybe a week or so, okay…but after that?

Margaret M. Stevens, in Claude Whitmyer's anthology *Mindfulness and Meaningful Work,* tells the following story:

> [There was] a man who died and found himself in a beautiful place, surrounded by every conceivable comfort. A white-jacketed man came to him and said, "You may have anything you choose: any food, any pleasure, and kind of entertainment."

The man was delighted, and for days he sampled all the delicacies and experiences of which he had dreamed on Earth. But one day he grew bored with all of it, and calling the attendant to him, he said, "I'm tired of all this. I need something to do. What kind of work can you give me?"

The attendant sadly shook his head and replied, "I'm sorry, sir. That's the one thing we can't do for you. There is no work here for you."

To which the man answered, "That's a fine thing. I might as well be in hell."

The attendant said softly, "Where do you think you are?"

This story gives new meaning to the old idea that each of us creates his own heaven or hell.

For Buddhism our real problem isn't inability to keep living forever. The more basic problem is right here and now: that our sense of self isn't real, which gives us, again, a sense of lack that manifests as insecurity and ungroundedness. Since we don't feel real enough, and nothing we acquire or achieve ever makes us feel real enough, we long for immortality as a kind of substitute reality that can postpone the problem indefinitely. Buddhism offers a different solution to that longing. To realize the true nature of the self is also to realize a liberating truth about time.

What's that truth? Time is not something I have, it's what "I" *am*. It turns out that (lack of) time itself was never the problem, but rather the false sense of a distinction between *me* and *"my" time*. Both sides of that duality are delusive, because each seems to exist separately yet actually they depend upon each other. To express their nonduality Zen Master Dogen coined the term *uji*—"being-time." My being and my time are not distinguishable.

Hui-k'o realized that there is no *me* to be found that is separate from the world I am *in*. In the same way, time is not something external to me. Instead of me being *in* space and time, it's more accurate to say that I am what space and time are doing, right here and now.

What's liberating about that? If I *am* time, then it makes no sense to say that I am trapped *in* time. Paradoxically, to *be* time is to be *free from* time, because time cannot constrain or contain me if it is not separate from me. What does that mean for how time is actually experienced? One way to express it is that my life/time is always present-tense. What is present is always changing, but it's always the present. When I remember what happened earlier I'm remembering *now*. When I plan for the future I'm planning *now*.

What is the difference between that kind of present and our normal understanding of the present? The *now* that I *have* immediately fades away into the past, moment by moment, but the *now* that I *am* never falls away to become the past, and is therefore the same as eternity. As the twentieth-century philosopher Ludwig Wittgenstein put it, "If by eternity we mean timelessness, then eternal life belongs to those who live in the present." An *eternal present*. I can realize this, however, only when that present is not haunted by my fear of death or sense of lack—which for most of us is rather rare. Usually we run away from the present because it is too uncomfortable.

Since this is not easy to understand, a couple thought-experiments may be helpful. Pick up a coffee or tea mug. Is the mug something that's *in* space, or is it a *form* that space takes? If the cup itself is separate from space, then we could imagine removing it from space— but what could this mean? A cup needs to be spatial to be a cup. A cup is a way of separating inside space (where the liquid goes) from outside space (where it shouldn't go). No space, no cup. The cup is what space is doing in that particular place.

Not only what space is doing in that particular place, but what space is doing in this particular moment, because it's the same with time. Time isn't something external to things that they just happen to be in. We might have a mental image of a timeless cup but the cups we drink from can't be removed from time. No time, no things. And, like cups, we too are not separate from our space and time. We are some of the forms that space-time (or being-time) takes. Another way to say it is that things (including us) are *processes* that are always spatial and temporal.

How does that make our lives eternal? Time for another spatial analogy. Think of a small island—a coral atoll, let's say—by itself in the middle of the sea, far from any other land. There is an ocean current, which flows steadily from west to east. How fast does that current flow? To measure its movement accurately, a fixed, unmoving perspective is needed, which the island provides. We could set up a device on the coral reef to measure the speed of the current as it flows past. But *what if there is no such unmoving perspective?* Suppose that, instead of being on an island, we were in a light rubber dinghy, which was moving along with the current, at the same speed as the current. How could we measure the speed of the current then? We couldn't. For us in the boat there would be no sense of a moving current. There's awareness of a current moving only if there is something else that's not moving. It's the relationship between the two perspectives that provides a sense of movement.

Again, it's the same with time. The fixed island is like our sense of self. The current is time, and we suffer because we fear that sooner or later our own current will stop. But the notion that there is something which doesn't move is a delusion, a mental-construction. As Buddhism emphasizes, everything is impermanent. Nothing has a "self-being" of its own apart from its time. All of us are actually part of the same current. My sense of self is composed of habitual ways of thinking, feeling, acting, and reacting—all of them being temporal processes, different forms that time takes.

If the flowing current includes everyone and everything, our normal understanding of time as something external to us is misleading. Often it's convenient to distinguish things from their time, but that is the relative truth. According to the ultimate truth, things can't really be distinguished from their temporality, and when they are nondual then time is really not different from eternity. The eternal present always stays the same—it's always *now!*—even as it always changes.

The Second Buddha

We say "*the* Buddha" because *Buddha* is a title, not a name. It means "the awakened one," or, even more literally, "the awake." What does that imply about the rest of us? We are sleeping, living in a dream, because we don't see the world as it actually is. It's as if our heads were surrounded by a fog or lens that distorts everything we perceive. What is that fog? Zen teachers talk about letting go of concepts, and Buddhism generally emphasizes the problems created by our craving and attachment. But can we be more specific about how that lens filters our experience and deceives us? When we understand how craving and language work together, we gain insight into how samsara, the world of suffering, is constructed—and how it can be deconstructed into an awakening that liberates us from the fog.

By no coincidence, understanding the role of language also gives us insight into what Nagarjuna was up to. Nagarjuna was an Indian Buddhist monk who lived sometime during the first few centuries C.E. He was a philosopher, in fact by general agreement the greatest of all Buddhist philosophers (if we grant that Shakyamuni himself was not a philosopher—a label he doubtless would have declined). In fact, Nagarjuna's writings are so important that he is sometimes called "the second Buddha." Unfortunately, they are also notoriously difficult to understand, which is why they are respected much more than they are actually studied. Today, however, Nagarjuna's work has attained a new significance, for he has become a major figure in the dialogue that has been developing between Buddhist and Western ways of thinking. That is mainly because Western philosophy has recently reached some remarkably similar conclusions, due to what is sometimes called its "linguistic turn." This involves a greater appreciation of how language affects the ways we experience the world—and ourselves.

We usually think of language (when we think of it at all) as something "transparent," or like a mirror that reflects things as they really are. The most important realization of twentieth-century Western philosophy was that language does not simply mirror the world: in fact, it largely determines what we notice and what we do not. One of the first Western philosophers to realize how language misleads us was Friedrich Nietzsche, who wrote:

> We do not only designate things with [words and concepts], we think originally that through them we grasp the true in things. Through words and concepts we are continually misled into imagining things as being simpler than they are, separate from one another, indivisible, each existing in and for itself. A philosophical mythology lies concealed in language that breaks out again every moment, however careful one may be otherwise.

Like Nagarjuna (and Buddhism generally), Nietzsche realized what this implies about the self: "The 'subject' is not something given, it is something added and invented and projected behind what there is."

That was pretty radical stuff for the Europe in the late nineteenth century. Later Western philosophers such as Ludwig Wittgenstein and Jacques Derrida developed this approach in their own ways. Yet Nietzsche's realization about language was nothing new to Buddhism. Nagarjuna, in particular, was demonstrating how language deceives us almost two thousand years ago, and the approach he developed, Madhayamaka, remains to this day the most important Mahayana philosophy (along with Yogachara, which eventually merged with it).

In his time Nagarjuna was a revolutionary—though he probably thought of himself more as a reformer. His innovations are firmly rooted in the original teachings of the Buddha, who refused to discuss metaphysical questions, such as whether the world had a beginning or not, or what happens to an enlightened person after death. Debating such issues is like someone struck by an arrow who refuses to be treated until he knows what wood the arrow is made of, who shot it, and so forth. Instead of offering a speculative explanation of the world, the Buddha's approach was pragmatic. He compared his Dharma to a raft, which we use to cross the river of life and death—but which we should not afterward carry everywhere on our backs.

Nagarjuna's approach might be called "linguistic therapy" in a double sense: it uses language to reveal how language deceives us. We think that we experience the real world, but the world as we understand it is a linguistic construct that deludes us. We get confused and suffer because we cling to our conceptual constructions as if they were the world itself. It turns out that our commonsense view of the world is not commonsense at all, because an unconscious philosophy is actually built into the ways we ordinarily use language. Nagarjuna's logic analyzes these ways of thinking in order to demonstrate that they are inconsistent and self-contradictory. By his own account, that is all he does. He does not try to replace our deluded ways of thinking with the *correct* way of thinking, for there is no correct understanding that we should identify with. Identifying with *any* conceptual understanding is what gets us into trouble. Instead, the true nature of things (including ourselves) becomes apparent when we let go of our delusions, including the ones embedded in ordinary language. Our emotional and mental turmoil is replaced by a serenity that cannot be grasped but can be lived.

Buddhism is "the Middle Way," yet that has meant different things at different times. The life of the Buddha shows a middle way between hedonism and asceticism. He taught a middle way between eternalism (the view that the self survives death) and annihilation-ism (the view that the self is destroyed at death): the middle way between them is not some halfway position but the fact that there is no self and never has been. Nagarjuna wrote about a middle position between being (things exist) and nonbeing (things do not exist). That middle way is *shunyata,* usually translated as "emptiness."

Shunyata does not mean non-existence, or a void, nor does it describe some transcendent reality such as God or Brahman. According to Nagarjuna *shunyata* simply refers to the fact that things have no "essence" or self-being of their own. All things arise and pass away according to causal conditions, which means they are dependent on other things that also arise and pass away. For Nagarjuna, *shunyata* is a concept that is useful because it can help us realize something, but which does not itself refer to something. *Shunyata* is a shorthand way to refer to this absence of self-existence. Yet the term is often misunderstood in one of two ways. For some people, *shunyata* means that nothing whatsoever exists, in any way, which amounts to nihilism. If nothing at all exists, there is no good reason to do anything (for example, following the Buddhist path), or not to do anything! This misses the fact that Nagarjuna's basic project is not an attempt to describe the world but analyzing and refuting the ways we (mis)understand the world—ways that involve language and craving working together.

Nagarjuna was scathing about a nihilistic understanding of *shunyata:* woe to those who hold it, for it's like grasping a snake by the wrong end. Such people confuse two different levels of truth, the relative (or conventional) and the ultimate (or absolute). The conventional is not ultimately true, but it's needed to point to the ultimate, and the concept of *shunyata* is one of the conventional truths that helps us realize the ultimate, which is something that cannot be expressed in words. In other words, *shunyata* is itself empty: it has meaning only in relation to something that is not-empty—that is, it is useful only for pointing out that things have no self-existence, to help pry us free from our attachment to things. Ultimately, there are no such things and therefore no *shunyata* either. We need to let go of the concept of *shunyata* too, just like the Buddha's raft.

Nagarjuna's "ultimate truth" does not refer to something that transcends this world, which is the other common misunderstanding of *shunyata*. As another Madhyamikan put it: "If you use reason to examine the conventional world as it appears to us, you can find nothing that is real [has self-existence]. That not-finding is itself the ultimate." That's all. There's nothing to attain, no correct understanding to be grasped.

Although Nagarjuna's writings address the philosophical controversies of his day, the theoretical positions he criticizes are based on our ordinary ways of thinking. In order to understand the world, we divide it up in various ways, especially into *things* and what they *do*: "The man ran." Another important distinction is between *things* and their *attributes*: "The man was tall." By no coincidence the first distinction reflects the basic linguistic difference between nouns and verbs (subjects and predicates), and the second one reflects another basic difference between nouns and adjectives. Why do we make those particular distinctions? How different might the world be for us if we didn't divide it up that way?

With language as our lens, we perceive the world as a collection of separate things that interact with each other in objective space and time. We separate things from each other by labeling them—that is, by giving them names. For example, the room I'm in right now, as I type these words, is full of things like books, chairs, a cup, a table, pens, papers, books and bookcases, lamps, as well as a floor (with rugs), walls (with door and window), ceiling, and so forth—

including myself, of course. Yet it's also a bit peculiar to understand myself as another object in the room, since "I" am in it in a different way than all those other things. What is that difference?

The problem with language—or rather, the problem with the ways we use language—isn't simply that it's how we divide up the world, by objectifying things using the nouns *books, chairs, a cup,* etc. Why are we so eager to do that? Because those words aren't just labels, they are *functions.* Naming helps me do things. When I know that something is a pen, I know what to do with it. Pens are usually not much of a problem, but suppose I'm addicted to wine. In that case, it may be quite important for me to be able to identify something as a wine bottle. The point is that language organizes the world into objects that have particular functions, which is necessary for me to seek them and become attached to them and use them to get other things I want. And one of those things with a particular function is *me.* What is my function? "I" am the one who uses all those other things. They exist for me to employ and enjoy. Yet this way of constructing the world into a sense-of-self inside (me) and separate objects outside (the rest of the world) plays an important role in causing *dukkha.*

When "I" was born I was given a name, and as I grew up I learned to think of myself as a "self-existing" thing similar in many ways to the other things I learned how to name. In this way I gained a sense of ongoing, permanent *identity* that persists through the various activities I *do.*

Yet we can't help noticing that things are impermanent. They originate and eventually disappear, because they are dependent upon conditions—which means, things depend upon each other, and change as those other things change. This is bad news for my sense of identity, caught between my sense of self as something that persists essentially unchanging, and the inevitable fate that awaits it. I distinguish myself from my actions and from the events that happen to me, including illness, old age, and death, the classic examples of suffering that inspired the Buddha's spiritual quest. In this way I also come to think of myself as separate from everyone and everything else, only to anticipate with dread the inevitable fate that awaits my separate self (as I understand it).

But what if that distinction is actually a delusion? Again and again, in different ways, Nagarjuna refutes this thought-constructed division between objects (especially *us*) and processes (what we *do*), by showing how that distinction can't account for causality, motion, perception, time, etc. In each case he demonstrates that seeing a difference between *things* and *what they do* (or *have*) is untenable, because once we have separated them we can't understand how they fit together. (The previous chapter discussed a good example, the distinction we usually make between myself and my time.) Our basic problem is that the "commonsense" way of understanding the world assumes this distinction, yet it's a distinction that does not objectively exist. We see the world that way—divided up between things and their activities—not because that's the way the world is but because that's how language works, distinguishing subjects from predicates, nouns from verbs and adjectives.

For example, consider the relationship between the *self* and its ever-changing mental and physical *states* (one's thoughts, beliefs, emotions, and bodily feelings). Is the self the same as those states, or different from them? The important point is that in everyday life we're constantly fudging the answer, because we go back and forth between them, sometimes acting as if they are the same, at other times distinguishing the self from its changing states. We say "I *am* (angry/hungry/tired)" and so forth, but we also have the sense of an "I" behind those states that persists unchanged; we believe the "I" that works is the same "I" that gets a paycheck at the end of the month. Which is true? A sense of self as something that both changes constantly yet stays the same is really a contradiction. Nagarjuna's explanation for that inconsistency is that the self is *shunya,* "empty."

In more modern terms, my *sense* of being a persistent, unchanging self is a construct.

What about nirvana? Awakening too is a *shunya* concept. Nirvana is not something objectively real, for the distinction we make between samsara and nirvana is another example of dualistic thinking that we project onto our experience. Instead, Nagarjuna refers to nirvana as "the end of *prapanca* (conceptual elaborations)," which includes the end of such dualistic ways of thinking. I experience the world as it really is when I let go of the ways of thinking that I am normally stuck in.

Nagarjuna never actually claims that "samsara is nirvana." Rather, he says that no difference can be found between them. The *koti* (boundary or range) of nirvana is the *koti* of samsara. The two terms simply refer to different ways of experiencing the world. Nirvana is not another realm or dimension but the deep peace experienced when our mental turmoil ends, because the objects that we have been trying to identify with—including the sense of self—are realized to be *shunya*. If things arise and pass away according to conditions, they have no reality of their own that we can cling to. Nagarjuna's most famous statement sums this up wonderfully: "*Shiva* [ultimate serenity] is the coming-to-rest of all ways of 'taking' things, the repose of named things. No truth has been taught by a Buddha for anyone anywhere." When we do not cling to names and concepts, we can experience things as they are. This includes Buddhist names and concepts, even the concept of nirvana and the very notion of "a Buddha."

In conclusion, if you understand what I've been saying, then you realize that all of it is (at best!) the "lower truth," something that is not to be undervalued, however, since (as Nagarjuna also emphasized) lower truths are needed to point to the "higher truth." Yet, as Wittgenstein put it, after you have climbed up the ladder you must kick it away. Fortunately, Buddhism is very good at helping us let go of such ladders.

How to Drive Your Karma

What are we going to do about karma? There's no point in pretending that karma hasn't become a problem for contemporary Buddhism. If we are honest with ourselves, most of us aren't sure how to understand it. Along with its twin, rebirth, karma has always been an essential Buddhist teaching, but we don't know how literally they should be interpreted. Karma is often taken as an impersonal and deterministic "moral law" of the universe, with a precise calculus of cause and effect comparable to Newton's laws of physics. This understanding, however, can lead to a severe case of "cognitive dissonance" for modern Buddhists, since the physical causality that modern science has discovered about the world seems to allow for no such mechanism.

Some important Buddhist teachings make more sense to us today than they did to people living at the time of the Buddha. What Buddhism has to say about *anatta* "not-self," for example, is consistent with what modern psychology has discovered about how the ego-self is constructed. Likewise, what Buddhist thinkers such as Nagarjuna have said about language—how it works, how it often misleads us—is consistent with what many linguists and philosophers have recently been emphasizing, and contemporary science agrees with Buddhist claims about interdependence (ecology) and insubstantiality (physics). In such ways Buddhism can fit quite nicely into modern ways of understanding. But not traditional views of karma. Of course, this by itself does not disprove anything. It does, however, encourage us to think more deeply about karma.

There are at least two other problems with the ways that karma has traditionally been understood. One of them is its unfortunate implications for many Asian Buddhist societies, where a self-defeating split has developed between the Sangha and the laity. Although the Pali Canon makes it quite clear that laypeople too can attain liberation, the main spiritual responsibility of lay Buddhists, as popularly understood today, is not to follow the path themselves but to support the monastics. In this way lay men and women gain *punna,* "merit"— a concept that commodifies karma. By accumulating merit they hope to attain a favorable rebirth, which for some offers the opportunity to become a *bhikkhu* next time. More often, though, lots of merit means rebirth into a wealthy family, if not winning the lottery this lifetime. This approach makes Buddhism into a form of "spiritual materialism," because Buddhist teachings are being used to gain material rewards.

Unavoidably, this has had a negative effect on the Sangha too. Visitors to Buddhist societies such as Thailand can be forgiven for concluding that the Sangha's main social role is not to teach the Dharma, or even to set a good example, but to serve as a "field of merit" that provides opportunities for laypeople to gain merit. According to popular belief, the more spiritually developed a *bhikkhu* is, the more merit a donation deposits into one's spiritual bank account. The most important thing for monastics, therefore, is to follow all the Vinaya rules and regulations strictly, and to be seen to do that, so that one is a worthy recipient of lay support. The result is that many Asian Sanghas and their lay supporters are locked into a co-dependent marriage where it's difficult for either partner to change. This preoccupation with karma is similar to the preoccupation of many Christians with sin—in fact they are mirror-images of each other. Sin is something negative to be absolved, whereas positive karma/merit is something to be sought and accumulated, yet psychologically they amount to the same thing: thus commodified, they are used to get a handle on our post-mortem destiny.

There is another issue that has important implications for how Buddhism will adapt to a more global role in the future. Karma has been used to rationalize racism, caste, economic oppression, birth handicaps, and everything else. Taken literally, karma justifies the authority of political elites, who therefore must deserve their wealth and power, and the subordination of those who have neither. It provides the perfect theodicy: if there is an infallible cause-and-effect relationship between one's actions and one's fate, there is no need to work toward social justice, because it's already built into the moral fabric of the universe. In fact, if there is no undeserved suffering, there is really no evil that we need to struggle against. It will all balance out in the end.

I remember a Buddhist teacher's reflections on the Holocaust in Nazi Germany during the World War II: "What terrible karma all those Jews must have had…" This kind of fundamentalism, which blames the victims and rationalizes their horrific fate, is something no longer to be tolerated quietly. It is time for modern Buddhists and modern Buddhism to outgrow it by accepting social responsibility and finding ways to address such injustices.

In the *Kalama Sutra,* sometimes called "the Buddhist charter of free inquiry," the Buddha emphasized the importance of intelligent, probing doubt. He said that we should not believe in something until we have established its truth for ourselves. This suggests that accepting karma and rebirth literally, without questioning what they really mean, may actually be unfaithful to the best of the tradition. This does not mean disparaging or dismissing Buddhist teachings about them. Rather, it highlights the need for modern Buddhism to *interrogate* those teachings. Given what is now known about human psychology, including the social construction of the self, how might we today approach these teachings in a way that is consistent with our own sense of how the world works? Unless we can do so, their emancipatory power will for us remain unrealized.

One of the most basic principles of Buddhism is interdependence, but I wonder if we realize what that implies about the original teachings of the Buddha. Interdependence means that nothing has any "self-existence" because everything is dependent upon other things, which are themselves dependent on other things, and so forth. All things originate and pass away according to causes and conditions. Yet Buddhism, we believe, originated in the unmediated experience of Shakyamuni Buddha, who became an "awakened one" when he attained nirvana under the Bodhi tree. Different Buddhist scriptures describe that experience in different ways, but for all Buddhist traditions his enlightenment is the basic source of all Buddhist teachings, which unlike Hindu teachings do not rely upon anything else such as the ancient revealed texts of the Vedas.

Although we usually take the above account for granted, there is a problem with it. That enlightenment story, as usually told, amounts to a myth of self-origination—something Buddhism denies! If the interdependence of everything is true for everything, the truth of Buddhism could not have sprung up independently from all the other spiritual beliefs of the Buddha's time and place (i.e., Iron-Age India), without any relationship to them. Instead, the teachings of Shakyamuni must be understood as a *response* to those other teachings, but a response that, inevitably, also *presupposed* many of the spiritual beliefs current in that culture—for example, popular Indian notions of karma and rebirth, which were becoming widespread at that time.

Consider the insightful comment that Erich Fromm made about another (although very different!) revolutionary, Sigmund Freud:

> The attempt to understand Freud's theoretical system, or that of any creative systematic thinker, cannot be successful unless

we recognize that, and why, every system as it is developed and presented by its author is necessarily erroneous....The creative thinker must think in the terms of the logic, the thought patterns, the expressible concepts of his culture. That means he has not yet the proper words to express the creative, the new, the liberating idea. He is forced to solve an insoluble problem: to express the new thought in concepts and words that do not yet exist in his language....The consequence is that the new thought as he formulates it is a blend of what is truly new and the conventional thought which it transcends. The thinker, however, is not conscious of this contradiction.

Fromm's point is that even the most creative and revolutionary thinkers cannot stand on their own shoulders. They too remain dependent upon their cultural context, whether intellectual or spiritual—which is precisely what Buddhist emphasis on impermanence and causal interdependence implies. Of course, there are important differences between Freud and Shakyamuni, but the parallel is nevertheless very revealing. The Buddha too expressed his new, liberating insight in the only way he could, using the religious categories that his culture could understand. Inevitably, then, his Dharma (or his way of expressing the Dharma) was a blend of the truly new (for example, teachings about *anatta* "not-self" and *paticca-samuppada* "dependent origination") and the conventional religious thought of his time (karma and rebirth). Although the new transcends the conventional, as Fromm puts it, the new cannot immediately and completely escape the conventional wisdom it surpasses.

By emphasizing the inevitable limitations of any cultural innovator, Fromm implies the impermanence—the dynamic, developing nature—of all spiritual teachings. In revolutionizing the spiritual path of his time the Buddha could not stand on his own shoulders, yet thanks to his profound insight those who followed could stand on his. As Buddhists, we tend to assume that the Buddha understood everything, that his awakening and his way of expressing that awakening are unsurpassable—but is that fair to him? Given how little we actually know about the historical Buddha, perhaps our collective image of him reveals less about who he actually was and more about our own need to discover or project a completely perfect being to inspire our own spiritual practice.

Another basic teaching of Buddhism is impermanence, which in this context reminds us that Hindu and Buddhist doctrines about karma and rebirth have a history, that *they have evolved over time.* Earlier Brahmanical teachings tended to understand karma mechanically and ritualistically. To perform a sacrifice in the proper fashion would invariably lead to the desired consequences. If those consequences were not forthcoming, then either there had been an error in procedure or the causal effects were delayed, perhaps until your next lifetime (hence implying reincarnation). The Buddha's spiritual revolution transformed this ritualistic approach to getting what you want out of life into a moral principle by focusing on *cetana,* "motivations, intentions." *Cetana* is the key to understanding how he ethicized karma. The *Dhammapada,* for example, begins by emphasizing the pre-eminent importance of our mental attitude:

> Experiences are preceded by mind, led by mind, and produced by mind. If one speaks or acts with an impure mind, suffering follows even as the cart-wheel follows the hoof of the ox.
>
> Experiences are preceded by mind, led by mind, and produced by mind. If one speaks or acts with a pure mind, happiness follows like a shadow that never departs.

To understand the Buddha's innovation, it is helpful to distinguish a moral act into three aspects: the *results* that I seek; the *moral rule or regulation* I am following (for example, a Buddhist precept or Christian commandment; also ritualistic procedures); and my mental attitude or *motivation* when I do something. Although these aspects cannot be separated from each other, we can emphasize one more than the others—in fact, that is what we usually do. By no coincidence, in modern moral philosophy there are also three main types of theories. *Utilitarian* theories focus on consequences, *deontological* theories focus on general principles such as the Ten Commandments, and *virtue theories* focus on one's character and motivations.

In the Buddha's time the Brahmanical understanding of karma emphasized the importance of following the detailed procedures (rules) regulating each ritual. Naturally, however, the people who paid for the rituals were more interested in the results. We have already noticed that, unfortunately, the situation in some Buddhist countries is not much different today. Monastics are preoccupied with following the complicated rules that regulate their lives, while laypeople are preoccupied with accumulating merit by giving gifts to them. Both of these attitudes miss the point of the Buddha's spiritual innovation, which emphasized the role of intention.

Nevertheless, some Pali Canon texts do support a largely deterministic view. (Is it a coincidence that most of these passages work to the material benefit of the Sangha that has preserved them?) For example, in the *Culakammavibhanga Sutra* (*Majjhima Nikaya* 135) karma is used to explain various differences between people, including physical appearance and economic inequality. However, there are other texts where the Buddha clearly denies moral determinism, for example the *Tittha Sutra* (*Anguttara Nikaya* 3.61) in which the Buddha argues that such a view denies the possibility of following a spiritual path:

There are priests and contemplatives who hold this teaching, hold this view: "Whatever a person experiences—pleasant, painful, or neither pleasant nor painful—that is all caused by what was done in the past."...Then I said to them, 'Then in that case, a person is a killer of living beings because of what was done in the past. A person is a thief...unchaste...a liar... a divisive speaker...a harsh speaker...an idle chatterer... greedy...malicious...a holder of wrong views because of what was done in the past." When one falls back on what was done in the past as being essential, monks, there is no desire, no effort [at the thought], "This should be done. This shouldn't be done." When one can't pin down as a truth or reality what should and shouldn't be done, one dwells bewildered and unprotected. One cannot righteously refer to oneself as a contemplative.

In another short sutra (*Sutta Nipata* 36.21), an ascetic named Shivaka asked the Buddha about the view that "'whatever a person experiences, be it pleasure, pain or neither-pain-nor-pleasure, all that is caused by previous action.' Now, what does the revered Gotama [Buddha] say about this?" To which the Buddha replies:

Produced by (disorders of the) bile, there arise, Shivaka, certain kinds of feelings....Produced by (disorders of the) phlegm...of wind...of (the three) combined...by change of climate...by adverse behavior...by injuries...by the results of karma—(through all that), Shivaka, there arise certain kinds of feelings....Now when these ascetics and Brahmins have such a doctrine and view that "whatever a person experiences, be it pleasure, pain or neither-pain-nor-pleasure, all that is caused by previous action," then they go beyond what they know by themselves and what is accepted as true by the world. Therefore, I say that this is wrong on the part of these ascetics and Brahmins.

While we take the words of the Buddha seriously, we should not overlook the humor of this passage. I can even imagine the Buddha passing wind, and then asking Shivaka, "Was *that* produced by karma?" Perhaps the important point to be gleaned from comparing such passages is that the earliest Buddhist teachings about karma are somewhat ambiguous. If they are insufficient by themselves as a guide for understanding karma today, I think that we should return to the Buddha's revolutionary emphasis on the motivations of our actions. How should we today appreciate the original insight of his approach?

The original Sanskrit term *karma* (*kamma* in Pali) literally means "action," while *vipaka* is the karmic result of action (also known as its *phala,* "fruit"). As this suggests the basic point is that our actions have consequences—more precisely, that our morally relevant actions have morally relevant consequences that extend beyond their immediate effects. In most popular understandings, the law of karma and rebirth is a way to get a handle on how the world will treat us in the future, which also implies, more immediately, that we must accept our own responsibility for whatever is happening to us now, as a consequence of something we must have done earlier. "If I was born blind, well, it must be my own fault." This misses the revolutionary significance of the Buddha's reinterpretation.

Karma is better understood as the key to spiritual development: *how our life-situation can be transformed by transforming the motivations of our actions right now.* When we add the Buddhist teaching about not-self—in modern terms, that one's sense of self is a mental construct—we can see that karma is not something the self *has,* it is what the sense of self *is,* and what the sense of self is changes according to one's conscious choices. "I" (re)construct myself by what "I" intentionally do, because "my" sense of self is a precipitate of habitual ways of thinking, feeling, and acting. Just as my body is composed of the food eaten, so my character is composed of conscious choices, for "I" am constructed by my consistent, repeated mental attitudes. People are "punished" or "rewarded" not for what they have done but for what they have become, and what we intentionally do is what makes us what we are. An anonymous verse expresses this well:

Sow a thought and reap a deed
Sow a deed and reap a habit
Sow a habit and reap a character
Sow a character and reap a destiny

What I do is motivated by what I think. Intentional actions, repeated over and over, become habits. Habitual ways of thinking, feeling, acting, and reacting construct and compose my sense of self: the kind of person I am. The kind of person I am does not fully determine what occurs to me but strongly affects what happens and how I respond to it.

Confession and repentance are so important because they are our way of acknowledging, both to others and to ourselves, that we are striving to not allow something we have done to become (or remain) a habitual tendency that forms part of our sense of self.

Such an understanding of karma does not necessarily involve another life after physical death. As the philosopher Spinoza expressed it in the last proposition of his *Ethics,* happiness is not the reward for virtue; happiness is virtue itself. We are punished not for our "sins" but by them. We become the kind of person who does that sort of thing.

To become a different kind of person is to experience the world in a different way. When your mind changes, the world changes. And when we respond differently to the world, the world responds differently to us. Insofar as we are actually nondual with the world, our ways of acting in it tend to involve feedback systems that incorporate other people. People not only notice what we do, they notice why we do it. I may fool people sometimes, yet over time my character becomes revealed as the intentions behind my deeds become obvious. The more I am motivated by greed, ill will, and delusion, the more I must manipulate the world to get what I want, and consequently the more alienated I feel and the more alienated others feel when they see they have been manipulated. This mutual distrust encourages both sides to manipulate more. On the other side, the more my actions are motivated by generosity, loving-kindness, and the wisdom of interdependence, the more I can relax and open up to the world. The more I feel part of the world and genuinely connected with others, the less I will be inclined to use others, and consequently the more inclined they will be to trust and open up to me. In such ways, transforming my own motivations not only transforms my own life; it also affects those around me, since what I am is not separate from what they are.

This more naturalistic understanding of karma does not mean we must necessarily exclude other, perhaps more mysterious possibilities regarding the consequences of our motivations for the world we live in. There may well be other aspects of karmic cause-and-effect that are not so readily understood. What is clear in either case, however, is that karma-as-how-to-transform-my-life-situation-by-transforming-my-motivations-right-now is not a fatalistic doctrine. Quite the contrary: it is difficult to imagine a more empowering spiritual teaching. We are not told to accept passively the problematic circumstances of our lives. Rather, we are encouraged to improve our spiritual lives and worldly situation by addressing those circumstances with generosity, loving-kindness, and nondual wisdom.

What's Wrong with Sex?

As Buddhism infiltrates the West, one of the important and interesting (of course!) points of contention is sexuality. Buddhism in Asia has been largely a cultural force for celibacy (among monastics) and sexual restraint, so how is Western Buddhism adapting to the sexual revolution?

Today many people in contemporary Western societies are sexually "liberated"—liberated, however, in a somewhat different fashion than the Buddhist tradition has usually understood liberation. We still have many problems with sex, but nowadays they are less likely to involve guilt and repression than various types of obsession such as addiction to pornography. Since the 1960s our lifestyles and customs have become very different from those with which patriarchal societies regulated sexual urges—often providing outlets for men while strictly controlling women and procreation. Our culture is saturated with sexuality, not only because sex is commodified in every possible way (being indispensable for grabbing our attention) but also because preoccupation with sexual gratification helps to fill up the void left by the collapse of any larger meaning. The importance of sex has ballooned because we are not sure what else is important in a God-less world that often seems intent on destroying itself.

This is not to demean the pleasures of sex, or the libidinal freedoms we enjoy today. Despite new kinds of social pressure, most of us benefit from many more options. The liberation of sexual preference means that gays, lesbians, bisexuals, and transsexuals can come out of the closet, leading to an important reduction in collective social *dukkha*. Premarital sex is more or less taken for granted, and marriage itself is no longer a matter of course. It has become a decision that many choose not to take, or to take and retake. Thanks to effective contraception, children too have become a matter of choice. Some people decry the self-centeredness of those who decide not to raise children, and some others decry the self-centeredness of those who do. Buddhism is unique among the major religions in not being pro-natalist. There is no doctrinal encouragement that we should have lots of children, which is another aspect of the Dharma to appreciate, given our overpopulation of the earth. The emphasis on monasticism works the other way, encouraging an alternative to procreation. The Buddha, like Jesus, was not a big proponent of "family values."

But how does Buddhism fit into our freewheeling ways today? Well, many of us aren't sure. Western monastics continue to follow the established regulations of their own tradition, or at least appear to do so (like some of their Asian counterparts, no doubt). However, most serious practitioners in the West, and probably in Asia, are lay. Since sexual morality is a matter of personal karma rather than God's commandment—"Do this or else!"—for the most part we continue to do what we want to do. And is there anything wrong with that?

The issue, I think, is not whether we should or shouldn't "be faithful" to the sexual customs of Asian Buddhist cultures. Instead, this is another opportunity to interrogate the Buddhist traditions: to ask why they had certain rules and guidelines about sex, which can help us determine how relevant those policies remain for us today. Needless to say, evaluating such an intimate topic is a delicate matter, yet such an examination cannot be avoided without risk of hypocrisy on the one side or merely yielding to established tradition on the other. We need to find the middle way between doing the same as premodern Buddhism, simply because that's what they did, and the other extreme that simply accepts what has become acceptable to many people today. It is the tension between these two perspectives that can be so illuminating. If Buddhism is to realize its liberative potential in our modern, globalizing world, such challenges cannot be evaded.

The rapid change in Western sexual morality has been uncomfortable for many, but for Buddhism the pelvic issues are mostly secular matters. The third precept is often translated as "sexual misconduct," which for laypeople is usually understood to exclude casual relations, "sex without commitment." Since the crucial concern for Buddhism is always *dukkha,* the most important thing is avoiding sex that harms others or causes them pain. That covers a lot of ground, yet it also leaves a lot of possibilities. There is no blanket prohibition of non-marital sex in the Pali Canon or its commentaries. One should not have sexual relations with someone married or engaged (to someone else), or with those who are under the protection of parents or guardians, but especially today many women (and men) do not fall into those categories, including sex workers. Although apparent tolerance of prostitution makes early Buddhism seem more broadminded than many modern Buddhists, this acceptance can also be understood as an aspect of patriarchy that we have outgrown, or should have outgrown.

There is, however, an important exception to this pelvic freedom. Abortion is killing. According to the Pali Canon, the Buddha said that it breaks the first precept to avoid killing or harming any sentient being. Any monastic who encourages a woman to have an abortion has committed a serious offense that requires expiation. We may wonder how much the Buddha knew about the genetic physiology of conception and pregnancy, but the textual prohibition is unambiguous. This absolute rule in early Buddhism is a source of discomfort and embarrassment to many Western Buddhists, and is often ignored by those who are aware of it. Abortion is common in some Asian Buddhist societies, perhaps most of all in Japan, where it has become widely accepted as a form of birth-control (partly because oral contraceptives were not legal until recently). Again, karma relativizes even this prohibition: to break the precept against harming others may create more suffering for yourself, yet that is your own decision—a flexibility precious to many liberal-minded Western Buddhists.

So can we conclude that, except for this exception of abortion, there is no problem reconciling basic Buddhist teachings about sex with our own proclivities today? It's not so simple, I think. There is another monastic offense that needs to be considered: the strict prohibition of sexual activity. Any *bhikkhu* whose penis enters a woman is "defeated" and expelled from the Sangha. (The rule is somewhat stricter for *bhikkhuni* nuns: any sexual activity is grounds for expulsion.) Of course, this prohibition does not apply to laypeople, so why should the rest of us be concerned about it? Because it raises issues that are relevant to anyone who is concerned to follow the Buddhist path.

First and foremost, we want to know why the rule is so absolute. In most ways, Buddhism is a very pragmatic religion (or, if you prefer, spiritual path). There is no God or god that must be obeyed, nor did the Buddha set himself up as one. In place of punishment for sin, our unskillful intentions and deeds accumulate bad karma: more suffering for ourselves. But if sexual activity is an offense it is usually a victimless crime. One moment of physical weakness and you are out of the Sangha for good—that's a heavy penalty to pay for a natural urge, isn't it?

In short, we shouldn't ignore this issue just because we are not monastics. The distinction between lay and monastic has become somewhat different in the West, and outside Asia today there are many more laypeople than monastics who are conscientiously practicing a meditative path aimed at awakening. What does it mean for us, then, that the Buddha strictly prohibited any sexual activity for his most serious and devoted followers? Understanding this issue may be crucial for our own spiritual development. It is not enough to say that "whatever the Buddha said is good enough for me." Since the Buddha himself was so pragmatic, we need to understand what is pragmatic about that strict rule, the better to preserve and practice his Dharma today—and sometimes the best way to preserve a teaching is by modifying it. To be true to Buddhism's own emphasis on impermanence and insubstantiality, maintaining the Dharma in very different times and places means we need to take into account what motivated the Buddha in his own time and place.

So, once again: why did Shakyamuni Buddha strictly prohibit sex for Sangha members? Evidently sexual purity was not an issue, as it has been for Catholicism, for example, with its emphasis on the Virgin Mary and the asexuality of Jesus. According to the New Testament, Jesus had no family of his own, but the Buddha had a wife and son, whom he deserted. The courtesan Ambapali was much respected for her gift of a mango grove to the Sangha; later she became a celibate *bhikkhuni* and after her awakening an esteemed teacher. The Buddhist tradition did not condemn or patronize her for her background as a high-class prostitute.

So what's the problem with sex?

Obviously sexual desire is a good example—the "best" example?—of *tanha,* "craving," which according to the four ennobling truths is the cause of *dukkha.* Nevertheless, we still want to know: is that because sex is somehow bad in itself, or is sex bad because it interferes in some way with the path to liberation? If the former, why is sexual activity intrinsically such an awful thing? The answer is not obvious, at least not to me. After all, our continuation as a species—not only physically but culturally, including spiritual traditions such as Buddhism—depends upon the reproduction of each generation. If, on the other hand, sex is bad because it interferes with following the path, precisely how does it obstruct? Is it a distraction? A bad habit? But then it's hard to see why a single offense is so serious: one strike and you're out.

Is it a physiological issue? According to the tantric traditions, it's important to sublimate sexual energy and direct it up the kundalini to the higher chakras, where it can blossom into enlightenment. That would make sexual activity unwise during periods of intense practice, when that energy is needed for other purposes, but not necessarily a bad thing during other times, such as after enlightenment, perhaps.

If craving is the cause of *dukkha,* however, isn't sexual desire incompatible with the deep serenity of nirvana? Even if unawakened monks still have such urges, it is important that they endeavor to live the dispassionate life that their practice is aiming at.

That may well be the most important reason, but I wonder if such an argument reflects the Theravada perspective better than the Mahayana. Mahayana emphasis that form is no other than emptiness (and vice-versa) challenges any duality between samsara (this world of *dukkha*) and nirvana. Nirvana is simply the true nature of this world, when our non-dwelling awareness is not fixated on particular forms...including attractive sexual ones. According to the Mahayana teachings, we should not reject form by dissociating it from our emptiness. Instead, awakening liberates us to dance freely with forms and between forms, without getting stuck on any. The difference is instructive. When a friend dies, for example, I might respond by dwelling in that quiet, empty place at my core where there is no life or death, no gain or loss, no joy or sadness. Yet I might also respond not by denying or resisting my feelings of grief but by "becoming one" with them and allowing the process of mourning to run its natural course, confident that I will not remain stuck there.

What does that difference in perspective imply about sexual desire? As we know all too well, it's very easy to get fixated on the object of our passion, or become obsessed with sexual pleasure generally.

Nonattachment to forms does not mean recommending promiscu-ity over monogamy (or vice-versa), for the issue is the relationship between one's non-dwelling awareness and sexual drive. According to the tantric tradition the energy of that urge can be used in a lib-erative way. Can attention retain awareness of its intrinsically non-attached nature, even while engaged in sexual activity? The normal tendency, of course, involves an increasingly urgent focus on the future release that is orgasm. In contrast, formless non-dwelling awareness is not driven to go anywhere or do anything, because it has nothing to gain or lose in itself. In climax, can one become more aware of that which does not climax, does not peak or decline? Fail-ure means becoming more entangled in the craving that leads to more *dukkha*. Success may mean freedom from addiction to pleas-ure, which is not the same as avoiding pleasure.

Such tantric practices are not found in the Pali sutras or in Ther-avada. Although the Theravada tradition should not be automatically identified with what the Buddha himself taught, its texts are the clos-est we get to those original teachings. Still, I can't help wondering if the puritanism found some places in the Pali Canon is an historical artifact, resulting from a general disparagement of the physical body that seems to have become common in India and elsewhere. The Axial Age that developed in several civilizations during the first millennium B.C.E. involved a stronger sense of transcendence, which included greater tension between that "higher world" and this material one. The duality between them opposed our immaterial spirit to the cor-ruptions of the flesh, denigrating nature, women, and sex—perhaps because they are associated with death? Our animal bodies remind us of our mortality...so let's make the soul immortal!

Such an explanation might help us understand some Pali Canon passages that seem excessive in the ways they disparage physical bod-ies as impure because they are composed of unattractive things such as urine, feces, pus, mucus, and so forth. A soul/body dualism doesn't quite fit Buddhism—on the contrary, Buddhism's emphasis on impermanence and not-self suggests a reaction against it—but such attitudes were apparently part of the cultural milieu the Buddha was raised in. Or did they arise afterward, and were inserted into the Canon later?

Whether or not such metaphysical considerations were a factor, other, more basic issues must have been important. Some of them are obvious and have already been mentioned. Monastic sexual activity would be a distraction, to say the least, and expend a lot of energy that would be better used in other ways. Think of how much time and effort sexual affairs and liaisons can involve, even when they are not secretive. Add to that all the tensions and jealousies that would be created within the Sangha.

Already it becomes apparent that having a more relaxed attitude toward sex would be fatal to the spiritual focus of the community. However, at least two other concerns must also have weighed heavily.

We tend to forget that until the 1960s there was really no reliable contraception. Since Buddhism prohibited abortion and infanticide, sex meant babies, and all the work of caring for them and raising them—especially the unremitting daily task of providing enough food, which is incompatible with a mendicant life. The consequences of this can be seen in the cautionary tale of Japanese Buddhism. Japanese culture has always viewed our natural urges as...well, natural. That very much includes the sexual urge, and many if not most temple monks had common-law wives and children before they were legally permitted to marry after the Meiji Restoration. The task of providing for them eventually transformed the temple into a family business, with the oldest son expected to become a priest to keep that temple business in the family, regardless of whether he had any religious inclinations. As a result, Japanese Buddhism today is a thriving (and lucrative) industry focusing on funerals and memorial services, and not much else.

One more factor may have been the most important of all. Buddhist monastics are traditionally dependent on lay support. This means that the Sangha must be very sensitive to the expectations of their supporters. For example, Chinese monks and nuns became vegetarian not because their vows required it but because the laity began to expect it. Also, needless to say, it wouldn't do to have monks seducing their supporters' daughters (or sons). Moreover, laymen and women would not look kindly upon sharing their hard-earned food and other resources with renunciants who, instead of devoting themselves to their spiritual practice, spend time dallying with lovers. Even today, when monks in southeast Asian countries like Thailand are discovered with girlfriends, it's sometimes the local lay community that takes the initiative in forcibly disrobing them.

To sum up, there are many strong reasons for the Buddhist Sangha to be strictly celibate. Which of these were the important factors? Early Buddhist texts do not help us decide among them, but my guess is that all of them were.

How does this list shed light upon our situation today? If it is more or less inclusive, there are major implications for Western Buddhism, because few if any of those reasons for celibacy are valid for lay practitioners today.

Yes, there are still times (periods of intensive practice) and places (within practice communities) when sexual abstention is obviously wise to observe. Few Western Buddhists, however, still look upon nature, women, and sex as impure entanglements to be avoided. Most of us don't have to worry about what our lay supporters think, because we don't have any, at least not in the traditional sense. Today we have access to effective means of birth-control, so babies usually aren't an issue unless and until we want them to be. A new category of Buddhist has become common in the West: less than monastic in lifestyle (hence not subject to Sangha vows or regulations) but also more devoted to practice than laity have usually been. This creates more distractions, since we must provide for ourselves, but most Western converts are middle-class folk able to find some balance between their careers and their Buddhist practice—that is, between periods when it is suitable to be celibate and times when that is not important.

So…does that mean we can breathe more easily now, as we accept and enjoy the new sexual freedoms? Not quite yet. There is another aspect of sexual relationships that we need to be aware of, and it's one that is not usually acknowledged.

Earlier I raised questions about soul/body dualism, and how it encouraged the devaluation of nature, our material bodies, women, and sexuality. Today it is easy for us to disparage such dualisms, which seem historically dated, but we should also become attentive to our own preconceptions. Our own cultural perspective should not be taken for granted, as if it provided some universal standard. Present Western attitudes are historically conditioned too, in this case by a myth about romantic love that evolved in late medieval Europe, originating in troubadour songs and the legend of Tristan and Isolde. Prior to that, European society, like most traditional societies, subordinated love to marriage, which was not merely a bond between individuals but a relationship between families, which is why the preferences of the young couple themselves were often not a decisive factor.

Despite what we are led to expect from all the media images that intrude upon us, traditional marriage is not primarily about sex but about babies. Pleasant though it be, the act of procreation is brief, while the activity of raising kids involves intense responsibility for many years. In the last couple generations the almost inevitable link between sex and babies has been somewhat severed, but most of us take for granted an important, if not essential, link between sex and personal happiness. Although some of the emphasis has shifted from finding the right spouse to finding the right sexual partner, there is still the same expectation of personal fulfillment whether through romance or sexual intimacy. Buddhism questions that conscious or unconscious expectation, just as it challenges other myths that predispose us to seek happiness—the end of *dukkha*—in an unskillful way.

Sexual intimacy is a source of pleasure and gratification, and a very nice one it can be; it can also help create and sustain deeper, more meaningful relationships. Nevertheless, the sex drive is basically biological. Sex is an appetite. We do not use our sexual organs; they use us. That is why there is ultimately something delusive about the myths of romantic love and sexual fulfillment. Sex is nature's way, and marriage is society's way, to reproduce the species. Genuine happiness—that is, the end of *dukkha*—for any of the parties involved has little if anything to do with it.

We don't like to hear this, and we don't want to believe it when we do. "Those intense feelings I have toward my partner make our physical and emotional bond *unique!* We are swept up in something wonderful that helps each of us transcend our individual sense of isolation and open up to something other than ourselves." Yes, your relationship is special, but that is simply because it is yours and not someone else's. It is part of the game that nature/biology/evolution plays with us, and if we don't understand this we are in for a fall and more *dukkha*.

The fall is the disillusionment that later occurs: the discouraging fact that, whether or not one marries, the relationship never quite works out to be as satisfying as expected, whether or not one eventually separates. We should recognize the uncomfortable truth that sex and romance cannot provide the long-term fulfillment—the end of *dukkha*—that we usually hope for from them. Sex is always nature's trick, and romance an emotional gloss on it. We anticipate that our partner will somehow make us feel complete, but that never happens, because no one else can ever do that for us.

The myth of romance encourages a delusive cycle of infatuation and disappointment followed by a different infatuation. The romantic high has faded? Then obviously he (or she) was not really the right one for me. Time to separate and try again with someone else!

This also helps us understand the painful transition that couples usually endure when they have children. The semi-official myth—a widespread social belief that no one dares to contradict publicly, or to warn new parents about—is that the great joy of having children brings mother and father closer together, as they beam down at their little offspring. The near-universal reality is that the unremitting stress of nuclear couples having and raising kids cannot but affect the relationship between the parents. The stronger the expectation of marital bliss, the greater the interpersonal difficulties—hence the high divorce rate among younger parents not yet mature enough to make the transition to a different type of child-centered relationship. (This is not to demean the joys of fatherhood!) To meet the persistent and ever-changing needs of young children, parents end up relating to each other mostly through the kids and their requirements. That's tough for those still trying to live the romantic myth.

Since babies are no longer inevitable, is that a reason for not having kids? Sometimes. Given the population crisis, we should think twice and thrice before we decide to reproduce. But sexual relationships tend to have a dynamic of their own, and—*surprise, surprise!*—the urge to have children becomes stronger as couples age and the woman's biological clock starts ticking more loudly. Mothers usually seem to make the transition more easily from focusing on the spouse to focusing on the baby, while many of us men have difficulty coping with that, especially the woman's reduced interest in sex. That change is also natural: sex isn't the biological process that needs to be emphasized anymore. Needless to say, however, none of this accords with the over-sexualized images of gratification that surround us today: Sex is the way to become happy!

None of this is an argument for celibacy or against sex, nor am I making an argument against (or for) marriage. Don't get me wrong: a committed sexual relationship between two people who cherish and trust each other can be a great joy. The issue is what we expect from our relationships. Without the myth of self-fulfillment through romance and/or sex, we would be less obsessed with sexuality and therefore suffer less whenever our expectations are frustrated. When we assume that sex is what can really make us happy, that my partner can and should complete me, we expect too much. Consciously or unconsciously we hope that romance and sex will fill up our sense of lack, but they don't and can't. The Buddhist path offers us a more effective way to resolve our *dukkha*.

What Would the Buddha Do?

Maybe every generation feels confronted by some crisis that will determine the fate of the world, but unless your head is buried in the sand (or some Buddhist equivalent) it's not possible to be ignorant of the extraordinary planetary crisis that confronts all of us today. Environmental collapse no longer merely threatens: we are well into it and it's already apparent that civilization as we know it is going to be transformed in some very uncomfortable ways by the mutually-reinforcing breakdown of ecological systems (due especially to global climate change), ozone depletion, rapid disappearance of many species, and various types of pollution, including some we probably don't know about yet.

Although our globalizing economic system is a wholly-owned subsidiary of the biosphere, most of the CEOs who direct this system (as much as anyone controls it) can't seem to plan much further than the next quarterly report, any more than politicians can think further than the next election. Overpopulation, pandemics, and the deprivation of basic necessities for vast numbers of people threaten social breakdown, while the media—profit-making enterprises whose primary focus is the bottom-line, rather than uncovering and revealing the truth—distract us with infotainment and assurances that the solution is more of the same. Keep the faith, hang in there long enough, and eventually technological development and economic growth, more consumerism and greater GNP, will resolve our problems.

As if that were not enough, our ignorant, corrupt, and arrogant leaders, or rather rulers, have shown themselves to be inept at almost everything except deception and gaining power. Now that their deceit and incompetence are coming back to haunt them, their popularity has been plummeting—but at the same time they have been consolidating their power. The faces will change while the power structure remains much the same, unless we find ways to do something about it.

One of the most important tools for maintaining their power is fear, which requires replacing the Cold War with a never-ending "war on terror" that means never-ending profits for a military-industrial complex that fattens on war and would collapse without it. Intentionally or not, the war on terror has been prosecuted in a way guaranteed to produce many more despairing people who hate the U.S., for every "terrorist" we kill. Our aggressive efforts to suppress terrorism ensure that it will continue. As Peter Ustinov put it, terrorism is the war of the poor; war is the terrorism of the rich. The violence of small terrorist groups such as al-Qaeda is, in the final analysis, trivial compared to the "state terrorism" (including sanctioned torture) that we feel justified in unleashing on anyone else who scares us or challenges our "national interests."

I do not offer the above reflections as political opinion but as fact. It is the critical situation we find ourselves in today, and Buddhists, like everyone else, need to face up to it quickly. To be quite blunt, if you are not at least dimly aware of these urgent problems, then you are living in some very strange bubble devoid of news (perhaps in the late stages of a twenty-year retreat in some Himalayan cave?), or there is a serious deficiency in your spiritual practice. Either you are not paying attention or something is wrong with your ability to see. I suspect there is a special place in hell (the Buddhist hells as well as the Christian one) reserved for those who refuse to give up the self-centered indifference that allows them to sit indefinitely on their cushions while the rest of the world goes to hell. Buddhism encourages mindfulness and awareness, and especially today it's necessary for that awareness to extend beyond our sitting cushions and Dharma practice halls, to embrace a broader understanding of what is happening in our world, to our world—a world that cries out in pain. Like Kwan Yin, we need to be able to hear that pain and to respond to it.

Sometimes we think that meditation practice means "just seeing, just hearing, just feeling is *good!*—concepts are *bad.*" There are times and places when we need to focus on immediate sensory and mental phenomena. Nevertheless, such practices are by themselves incomplete, like a Buddhist awakening that liberates us without also motivating us to address the liberation of everyone. Otherwise we may end up like frogs at the bottom of a deep well, oblivious to the wider world that exists outside. If your Buddhist practice makes you allergic to all concepts and abstractions, then you'd better be prepared to visit the South Pole to experience directly your own ozone-hole sunburn, and the arctic tundra to wallow personally in the melting permafrost mud, and the slums of Bogotá and Rio de Janeiro to see for yourself how families survive there, and Baghdad to learn for yourself what "bringing democracy to the Middle East" means on the ground…and a lot of other places as well, in order to become aware of what is happening in the world right now.

Those of us who do not have the time, money, or energy for such travel need to develop wider awareness in other ways, ways that do not rely on junk media or Washington spin machines. We must employ our critical faculties to understand the enormous challenges facing the world we live in. *Concepts and generalizations are not bad in themselves,* and rejecting them entirely is like blaming the victim, for the problem is the ways we misuse them.

Believing that mindfulness means attentiveness only to my immediate surroundings, and placing such limits on our awareness, is really another version of the basic problem: our sense of separation from each other and from the world we are "in." *Anatta,* "not-self," means that it is delusive to distinguish "my own best interests" from what is in the best interest of everyone. As the law of karma implies, the world is not that kind of zero-sum game.

There are two other common Buddhist responses that try to justify focusing solely on one's own practice and enlightenment: "I must tend to my own liberation before I can be of service to others" and "From the highest point of view there are no living beings—everything is 'empty'—so we needn't worry about their fate, or that of the biosphere." Neither of these answers will do, however, because in different ways they are both dualistic half-truths at best.

To begin with, we can't wait until we have overcome all our own suffering before addressing others' suffering, because the world is speeding up, and events are not going to wait for you and me to attain great enlightenment. Since the degrees of enlightenment are infinite (even the Buddha is only halfway there, according to a Zen saying), we need to contribute whatever we can here and now. More precisely, we need to do what we can according to *where we are in our practice* right now.

Furthermore, this objection misunderstands how spiritual practice works. We don't wait until we overcome our self-centeredness before engaging with the world; addressing the suffering of the wider world is *how* we overcome our self-centeredness. Contrary to a common way of understanding the bodhisattva path, bodhisattvas don't defer their own perfect enlightenment in order to help others; helping others is how they perfect their enlightenment, because they know that their own liberation ultimately cannot be distinguished from others. We awaken from our own self-suffering to discover a world full of suffering. To awaken is to realize that *I am not other than that world.*

But it's all empty, right? Yes and no. To focus solely on the emptiness aspect is to dichotomize again and misunderstand the essential teaching of Mahayana. Form is emptiness, but emptiness is also form. Phenomena have no essence, yet our formless, non-dwelling essential nature manifests only in one form or another. Without manifestations it remains nothing, amounts to nothing, and has no meaning. Not to cherish the intricate web of life that the earth has miraculously spun—including us, deluded as we are—is to denigrate the wondrous activity of the essential nature that we share with all other beings. Enlightenment is not about attaining some higher reality or transcendental state of consciousness, it is realizing our essential oneness with the world (which is the same as realizing the emptiness of our self-being) and acting accordingly. Without a healthy biosphere, the possible forms available to emptiness are much diminished. Without healthy societies, the possibilities for fulfilling human activity, including the path to enlightenment, are damaged.

So: What would the Buddha do? How would he respond to our situation?

I sometimes wonder what he would think about "Buddhism" today. The Buddha never taught Buddhism; we can even say that he was not a Buddhist, in the sense that Jesus was never a Christian. Shakyamuni taught the "Dhamma." Buddhism isn't what the Buddha taught; it's what the Buddha began. Buddhism as we know it is how the Dhamma (Dharma) and Sangha developed over the centuries, in many different places and cultures. Would he be pleased with what his efforts begat?

His teachings emphasize impermanence and insubstantiality. He wouldn't be surprised by the history of constant change, or by the extraordinary adaptability that Buddhism has demonstrated wherever it has spread. He wouldn't expect us to simply follow and repeat his ways of teaching, nor to stick to all the rules that evolved for regulating the Sangha in his day. Surely he would not want us to remain unaware of the challenges that face us collectively, nor would he expect his followers to ignore them. In his time Sangha members could sometimes disregard political struggles and social conflict by withdrawing back into the forest. Today there is nowhere on earth to hide that is not under some threat. The traditional duality between lay and ordained does not apply in this situation. Our fates cannot be distinguished.

What would the Buddha do? Is the answer that we can't know, because he's not here? If the Buddha doesn't live in us and as us, he is indeed dead. If we are unable to answer that question for ourselves, Buddhism is dead—or might as well be. The challenge for you and me is determining how to apply the most important Buddhist teachings to our present situation. If those teachings do not work for understanding and addressing the global crises we face today, so much the worse for those teachings; maybe it's time to replace them.

Of course, I do not think that is what is called for. The most distinctive Buddhist teaching is also the one that gives us the most insight into the collective crises confronting us: the relationship between *dukkha* and *anatta,* between suffering (in the broadest sense) and the delusive sense of self. A sense of self is inevitably uncomfortable since, being a psychological construct, it is groundless, and the usual ways it tries to ground itself to feel more "real" just make things worse. This essential truth about the individual self is just as revealing about "collective selves," which also try to secure themselves by promoting their own group self-interest at the price of those outside. This gets to the heart of why sexism, racism, nationalism, militarism, and species-ism (the alienation between human beings and the rest of the biosphere) are self-defeating. If sense of separation is the problem, embracing interdependence must be at the heart of any solution. Our rulers are failing so miserably because their policies embody and reinforce the delusion of separation, which is why they keep aggravating the world's *dukkha* rather than alleviating it.

Such interdependence is not merely an insight to be cultivated on our cushions. A suffering world calls upon us to truly *realize* interdependence—to make it real—in the ways we actually live. If we Buddhists do not want to do this or cannot find ways to do this, then Buddhism is not the spiritual path that the world needs today.

The Three Poisons, Institutionalized

Shakyamuni, the historical Buddha, lived at least 2,400 years ago. Buddhism began as an Iron Age religion and all its teachings are pre-modern. So can Buddhism really help us understand and respond to contemporary social problems such as economic globalization and biotechnology, war and terrorism (and the war on terrorism), climate change and other ecological crises?

What the Buddha understood is human *dukkha:* how it works, what causes it, and how to end it. *Dukkha* is usually translated as "suffering," but as previous chapters have discussed it's better understood as a basic dis-ease, for it is the nature of our unawakened minds to be bothered about something. The fundamental insight of Buddhism is the connection it emphasizes between such *dukkha* and the self. My deepest frustration is caused by my sense of being a self that is separate from the world I am in. This sense of separation is illusory—in fact, it is our most dangerous delusion.

What does this imply about *collective* selves? Don't we also have a group sense of separation between ourselves "inside" and the rest of the world "outside"? And if my individual sense of self is the root source of my *dukkha,* because I can never feel secure enough, do collective senses of self also mean that there is such a thing as collective *dukkha?* A collective sense of *lack*?

In fact, many of our social problems can be traced back to such a group ego, when we identify with our own race, nationality, religion, etc., and discriminate between ourselves and another group.

Historically this has been a perpetual problem, but in some ways our present situation has become quite different from that of Shakyamuni Buddha. Today we have not only much more powerful scientific technologies but also much more powerful social institutions. We not only have group egos; there are institutionalized egos.

From a Buddhist perspective, the problem with modern institutions is that they *tend to take on a life of their own as new types of collective ego.* Consider, for example, how a big corporation works. Even if the CEO of a transnational company wants to be socially responsible, he or she is limited by the expectations of stockholders. If profits are threatened by his sensitivity to environmental concerns, he is likely to lose his job. Large corporations are new forms of *impersonal* collective self, which are very good at preserving themselves and increasing their power, quite apart from the personal motivations of the individuals who serve them. John Ralston Saul, in *The Doubter's Companion,* describes this as the "amorality" of modern organizations:

> **AMORALITY**: A quality admired and rewarded in modern organizations, where it is referred to through metaphors such as professionalism and efficiency....Immorality is doing wrong of our own volition. Amorality is doing it because a structure or an organization expects us to do it. Amorality is thus worse than immorality because it involves denying our responsibility and therefore our existence as anything more than an animal.

We human beings have a propensity to do the most awful things if we think that the responsibility for them belongs to someone else. We're just doing our jobs.

There is another Buddhist principle that can help us understand this connection between collective selves and collective *dukkha:* the three unwholesome motivations, also known as the three poisons—

greed, ill will, and delusion. The Buddhist understanding of karma emphasizes the role of these motivations, because one's sense of self is composed largely of habitual intentions and the habitual actions that follow from them. Instead of emphasizing the duality between good and evil, Buddhism distinguishes between wholesome and unwholesome *(kusala/akusalamula)* tendencies. Negative intentions reinforce the sense of separation between myself and others. That is why they need to be transformed into their more wholesome and nondual counterparts: greed into generosity, ill will into loving-kindness, and delusion into wisdom.

That brings us to a very important question for socially engaged Buddhism: Do the three poisons also operate collectively? If there are collective selves, does that mean there are also collective greed, collective ill will, collective delusion? To ask the question in this way is to realize the answer. Our present economic system institutionalizes greed, our militarism institutionalizes ill will, and our corporate media institutionalize delusion. To repeat, the problem is not only that the three poisons operate collectively but that they have taken on a life of their own. Today it is crucial for us to wake up and face the implications of these three institutional poisons.

Institutionalized Greed. Despite all its benefits, our economic system institutionalizes greed in at least two ways: corporations are never profitable enough, and people never consume enough. To increase profits, we must be conditioned into finding the meaning of our lives in buying and consuming.

Consider how the stock market works. It tends to function as an ethical "black hole" that dilutes the responsibility for the actual consequences of the collective greed that now fuels economic growth. On the one side of that hole, investors want increasing returns in the form of dividends and higher share prices. That's all that most of them care about, or need to care about—not because investors are bad people, but because the system doesn't encourage any other kind of responsibility. On the other side of that black hole, however, this generalized expectation translates into an impersonal but constant pressure for profitability and growth, preferably in the short run. The globalization of corporate capitalism means that this emphasis on profitability and growth are becoming increasingly important as the engine of the world's economic activity. Everything else, including the environment and the quality of life, tends to become subordinated to this anonymous demand for ever-more profit and growth, a goal that can never be satisfied. The biosphere is converted into "resources," and people into "human resources."

Who is responsible for the pressure for growth? That's my point: the system has attained a life of its own. We all participate in this process, as workers, employers, consumers, investors, and pensioners, with little if any personal sense of moral responsibility for what happens. Such awareness has been diffused so completely that it is lost in the impersonal anonymity of the corporate economic system. In other words, greed has been thoroughly institutionalized.

Institutionalized Ill Will. Many examples of institutionalized ill will spring to mind: racism, a punitive judicial system, the general attitude toward undocumented immigrants—but the "best" example, by far, is the plague of militarism. In the twentieth century at least 105 million people, and perhaps as many as 170 million, were killed in war, most of them non-combatants. Global military expenditures, including the arms trade, amounted to the world's largest expenditure in 2005: well over a trillion dollars, about half of that spent by the U.S. alone. To put this in perspective, the United Nations spends only about $10 billion a year. The United States has been a militarized society since World War II, and increasingly so.

Most recently, the second Iraq War, based on lies and propaganda, has obviously been a disaster, even as the war on terror has been making all of us less secure, because every "terrorist" we kill or torture leaves many grieving relatives and outraged friends. Terrorism cannot be destroyed militarily because it is a tactic, not an enemy. Again: if war is the terrorism of the rich, terrorism is the war of the poor and disempowered. We must find other ways to address its root causes.

The basic problem with war is that, whether we are "the good guys" or "the bad guys," it promotes and rationalizes the very worst part of ourselves: we are encouraged to kill and brutalize other human beings. (In one sense—the most important sense?—once a war begins there are no good guys or bad guys, just groups of people trying to hurt other groups of people.) In doing these things to others, though, we also do them to ourselves. This karma is very simple. To brutalize another is to brutalize myself—that is, to become the kind of person who brutalizes.

This is the sort of behavior we would never do by ourselves, except for a very small number who receive our heaviest social retribution. In war, however, such behavior is sanctioned. Why? Because it is always justified as collective self-defense. We all accept the right and necessity to defend ourselves, don't we? If someone invades my home and attacks me, it's okay to hurt them in self-defense, even kill them, if necessary. War is national self-defense, and, as we know all too well today, national defense can be used to rationalize anything, including torture and what is euphemistically called "preventive war." And just because we ourselves are not the soldiers sent overseas to do the dirty work does not mean that we remain innocent of the consequences. As Abraham Heschel used to say, some are guilty but all are responsible. Our society as a whole is responsible, and we are part of that society.

It's curious that our national self-defense requires us to have at least 737 (the official number in 2005) overseas military installations, in 135 countries. It turns out that, in order to defend ourselves, we have to dominate the rest of the world. While we insist that other nations do not develop nuclear weapons, we spend almost $18 billion a year to maintain and develop our own stockpile, today equivalent to about 150,000 Hiroshima-size bombs. (Since 1997 the U.S. has conducted 23 "subcritical" nuclear tests to help design new nuclear weapons.) Using even two or three percent of those bombs would end civilization as we know it! No matter how hard we try, no matter how many weapons we have, it seems like we can never feel secure enough—just like our GNP can never be big enough.

In sum, our huge military-industrial complexes institutionalize ill will. Our collective negativity has taken on a life of its own, with a self-reinforcing logic likely to destroy us all if we don't find a way to subvert it.

Institutionalized Delusion. The Buddha is literally "the awakened one," which implies that the rest of us are unawakened. We live in a dream-like world. How so? Each of us lives inside an individual bubble of delusions that distorts our perceptions and expectations. Buddhist practitioners are familiar with this problem, yet we also dwell together within a much bigger bubble that largely determines how we collectively understand the world and ourselves. The institution most responsible for molding our collective sense of self is the media, which have become a kind of "group nervous system." Genuine democracy requires an independent and activist press, to expose abuse and discuss political issues. In the process of becoming megacorporations, however, the major media have abandoned all but the pretence of objectivity.

Since they are profit-making institutions whose bottom-line is advertising revenue, their main concern is to do whatever maximizes those profits. It is never in their own interest to question the grip of consumerism. We will never see a major network TV series about a happy family that decides to downsize and live more simply so they can have more time together. Thanks to clever advertisements, my son can learn to crave Nike shoes and Gap shirts without ever wondering about how they are made. I can satisfy my coffee and chocolate cravings without knowing about the social conditions of the farmers who grow those commodities for me, and without any awareness of what is happening to the biosphere.

An important part of genuine education is realizing that many of the things we think are natural and inevitable (and therefore should accept) are in fact conditioned (and therefore can be changed). The world doesn't need to be the way it is; there are other possibilities. The present role of the media is to foreclose most of those possibilities by confining public awareness and discussion within narrow limits. With few exceptions, the world's developed (or "economized") societies are now dominated by a power elite composed of the government and large corporations including the major media. People move seamlessly from each of these institutions to the other because there is little difference in their worldview or their goals— primarily economic expansion. Politics remains "the shadow cast by big business over society," as John Dewey once put it. The role of the media in this unholy alliance is to "normalize" this situation, so that we accept it and continue to perform our required roles, especially the frenzied production and consumption necessary to keep the economy growing.

It's important to realize that we are not simply being manipulated by a clever group of people who benefit from that manipulation. Rather, we are being manipulated in a self-deluded way by a group of people who (mistakenly) think they benefit from it—because they also buy into the root delusion that their ego-selves are separate from other people. They too are victims of their own propaganda, caught up in the larger webs of collective illusion that include virtually all of us. (The Austrian writer Karl Kraus: "How do wars begin? Politicians tell lies to journalists, then believe what they read in the newspapers.")

According to Buddhism samsara is not only a world of suffering, it is just as much a world of delusion, because delusions are at the root of our suffering. That includes collective fantasies such as the necessity of consumerism and perpetual economic growth, which requires collective repressions such as denial of global climate change.

Realizing the nature of these three institutionalized poisons is just as important as any personal realization we might have as a result of spiritual practice. In fact, any individual awakening we may have on our meditation cushions remains incomplete until it is supplemented by such a "social awakening." Usually we think of expanded consciousness in individual terms, but today we must dispel the bubble of group delusion to attain greater understanding of dualistic social, economic, and ecological realities.

If this parallel between individual *dukkha* and collective *dukkha* holds, it is difficult to avoid the conclusion that the great social, economic, and ecological crises of our day are also *spiritual* challenges, which therefore call for a response that must also have a spiritual component.

Consciousness Commodified: The Attention-Deficit Society

Do we fail to see the nature of liberated mind, not because it is too difficult to understand, but because it is too obvious? Maybe we cannot find what we are searching for because it is in plain sight, like the spectacles that rest unnoticed on my nose.

According to the seventeenth-century Japanese Zen master Hakuin, the difference between Buddhas and other beings is like that between water and ice. Without water there is no ice, without Buddha no sentient beings—which suggests that deluded beings are simply "frozen" Buddhas. "Let your mind come forth without fixing it anywhere," says the most-quoted line from the *Diamond Sutra,* which prompted the great awakening of the sixth Chan patriarch Huineng, whose *Platform Sutra* makes and remakes the same point. "When our mind works freely without any hindrance, and is at liberty to 'come' or to 'go,' we attain liberation." Such a mind "is everywhere present, yet it 'sticks' nowhere." A mind that dwells upon nothing is the unborn Buddha-mind itself, according to Chan master Huihai: "This full awareness in yourself of a mind dwelling upon nothing is known as having a clear perception of your own mind, or, in other words, as having a clear perception of your own nature."

They are pointing to the same realization:

Delusion (ignorance, samsara): attention/awareness is fixated
(attached to forms)
Liberation (enlightenment, nirvana): attention/awareness is
liberated from grasping

Although the true nature of awareness is formless, it becomes
trapped when we identify with particular forms. Such identifications
happen due to ignorance of the essential "non-dwelling" nature of
our attention.

We are familiar with such teachings, yet an important implication
is not usually considered: the danger of what might be called *collective attention-traps*. Meditation practices make me more sensitive to
my attachments: the places where my awareness is stuck. But my
problems with attachment are not just my own. We tend to have the
same problems because as members of the same society we are subjected to similar conditioning and so tend to get stuck in similar
ways. How different is our present conditioning from social conditioning in the time of the Buddha, and in other Asian Buddhist societies? How has the development of the modern/postmodern world
affected human attention generally? Not only *what* we attend to, but
how we attend to it. The constriction or liberation of awareness is
not merely a personal, individual matter. What do contemporary
societies do to encourage or discourage its emancipation?

These questions are important because today our awareness is
conditioned in at least three new ways that did not afflict previous
Buddhist cultures and practitioners.

The Fragmentation of Attention. Media coverage suggests that one of
our major concerns about attention is the lack thereof. Attention-deficit disorder (ADD) and attention-deficit hyperactivity disorder
(ADHD) have become a serious medical issue in the U.S., originally
among schoolchildren but now among young adults as well.

According to the *New York Times,* the use of drugs to treat attention-deficit disorder in young adults doubled between 2000 and 2004, to one percent of adults under 65, and the share of children using such drugs increased to almost five percent, despite mounting concern about their side-effects. What are we to make of this?

Buddhist practice evokes images of meditation with minimal distractions. The "IT revolution"—personal computers, the Internet, email, cell phones, and iPods, etc.—encourages an unremitting connectivity that pulls us in the opposite direction. As we become attentive to so many more people and so many more possibilities always available, is less attention available for the people and things most important to us?

Consider, for example, how MP3 players are changing the ways we listen to music. A century ago, you are part of a live audience, and once you are there you are *there,* so you settle down and focus on the music being performed. For me today, strolling along with my iPod, the decision to listen to any particular "selection" is never completely settled in the sense that I can instantaneously change what is playing if I become dissatisfied with it, for any reason at any time, simply by pressing a button. I must, in effect, continually decide to listen to this particular song. Does awareness of these other possibilities distract my attention from the music I am actually hearing?

Of course, this point applies just as much to many other aspects of our lives: TV channel-surfing, the surfeit of books and DVDs (obtained via Amazon *One-Click* orders!), video-games, surfing the net, etc. Our old mental foraging habits were based on info-scarcity, but suddenly, like Mickey Mouse as the sorcerer's apprentice, we find ourselves trying to survive an *info-glut,* and the scarcest resources have become *attention* and *control over our own time.* The Swedish scholar of information technology Thomas Eriksen has formalized this relationship into a general law of the information revolution: "When an ever-increasing amount of information has to be squeezed into the relatively constant amount of time each of us has at our disposal, the span of attention necessarily decreases."

One problem with such an avalanche of information (and therefore shorter attention spans) is that it challenges our ability to construct narratives and logical sequences. The MIT professor Sherry Turkle has noticed that some of her students now reason and arrange their ideas differently. "There is this sense that the world is out there to be Googled," she says, "and there is this associative glut. But linking from one thing to another is not the same as having something to say. A structured thought is more than a link."

In place of the usual Buddhist warnings about clinging and attachment, many of us now have the opposite problem: an inability to concentrate. Yet, as we know all too well from our meditation practices, an attention that jumps from this to that, unable to focus itself, is no improvement over an awareness that is stuck on something.

The Commodification of Attention. For most of us in the developed world, the greatest "awareness trap" is consumerism, which involves sophisticated advertising that has become very good at manipulating our attention. Today the big economic challenge is not production but keeping us convinced that the solution to our *dukkha* is our next purchase. According to the pioneering advertising executive Leo Burnett, good advertising does more than circulate information. "It penetrates the public mind with desire and belief." That penetration may have been lucrative for his clients, but there are other consequences, as Ivan Illich pointed out: "in a consumer society there are inevitably two kinds of slaves, the prisoners of addiction and the prisoners of envy." Whether or not one is able to afford the desired product, one's awareness is captured.

Recently it has become more evident that attention is the basic commodity to be exploited. Ben Franklin's old adage needs to be updated: not *time is money* but *attention is money*. According to

Jonathan Rowe's article "Carpe Callosum," the key economic resource of this new economy is not something they provide, it's something we provide—"mindshare," to use the new idiom. But, he asks, "What if there's only so much mind to share? If you've wondered how people could feel so depleted in such a prosperous economy, how stress could become the trademark affliction of the age, part of the answer might be here."

A turning point in the development of capitalism was "the enclosures" in sixteenth- and eighteenth-century Britain, when villagers were forced out of their traditional villages because landlords could make more money raising sheep. Rowe discusses "the ultimate enclosure—the enclosure of the *cognitive commons,* the ambient mental atmosphere of daily life," a rapid development now so pervasive that it has become like the air we breathe unnoticed. Time and space have already been reconstructed: holidays (including new commercialized ones such as Mother's Day) into shopping days, Main Street into shopping malls. Advertising is infiltrating into every corner of our conscious (and unconscious) awareness. Sports stadiums used to have ads; now renamed stadiums are themselves ads. TV shows used to be sponsored by ads; today product placement makes the whole show (and many movies) an ad. The jewelry company Bulgari sponsored a novel by Fay Weldon that included over three dozen references to its products. A 2005 issue of the *New Yorker* did not include any ads because the whole magazine was a promotion for the retail chain Target. Children are especially vulnerable, of course, and while half of four-year-old children do not know their own name, two-thirds of three-year-olds recognize the golden arches of McDonald's.

In the past one could often ignore ads, but enclosure of the cognitive commons means they now confront us wherever our attention turns. Unless we're meditating in a Himalayan cave, we have to process thousands of commercial messages every day. As Rowe emphasizes, they do not just grab our attention, they exploit it:

The attention economy mines us much the way the industrial economy mines the earth. It mines us first for incapacities and wants. Our capacity for interaction and reflection must become a need for entertainment. Our capacity to deal with life's bumps and jolts becomes a need for "grief counseling" or Prozac. The progress of the consumer economy has come to mean the diminution of ourselves.

Consumerism requires and develops a sense of our own impoverishment. By manipulating the gnawing sense of lack that haunts our insecure sense of self, the attention economy insinuates its basic message deep into our awareness: the solution to any discomfort we might have is consumption. Needless to say, this all-pervasive conditioning is incompatible with the liberative path of Buddhism.

The Control of Attention. Dictatorships control people with violence and the threat of it, to restrain what they do. Modern democracies control people with sophisticated propaganda, by manipulating what they think. The title of one of Noam Chomsky's books sums it up well: *Manufacturing Consent.* We worry about weapons of mass destruction, but we should be as concerned about weapons of mass deception (and weapons of mass distraction), which may be more insidious and more difficult to detect. To cite only the most obvious example, the disastrous 2003 invasion of Iraq would never have been possible without carefully orchestrated attempts to make the public anxious about weapons that did not exist. It was easy to do because 9/11 has made us fearful, and fearful people are more susceptible to manipulation.

Traditionally rulers and ruling classes used religious ideologies to justify their power. In pre-modern Europe the Church supported the "divine right" of kings. In Asian Buddhist societies karma offered a convenient way to rationalize both the ruler's authority and the powerlessness of his oppressed subjects. You should accept your present social status because it is a consequence of your past deeds. In modern secular societies, however, acquiescence must be molded in different ways.

According to the Australian scholar Alex Carey, the twentieth century was characterized by three important political developments: the growth of democracy, the growth of corporate power, and the growth of propaganda as a way protect corporate power against democracy. Although corporations are not mentioned in the Constitution—the Founding Fathers were wary of them—corporate power began to expand dramatically toward the end of the nineteenth century, so successfully that today there is little if any effective distinction between major corporations and the federal government. Both identify wholeheartedly with the same goal of continuous economic growth, regardless of its social or ecological effects. (We are repeatedly told that any unfortunate consequences from this growth obsession can be solved by more economic growth.) This often requires foreign intervention, for our access to resources and markets must be protected and expanded, usually under the guise of "defending ourselves." In effect, we have only one major political party: the Business Party, with two different faces that promote much the same agenda.

Continual economic growth requires that we define ourselves primarily as workers and consumers, while accepting that our present government and economy are "the best in the world." Instead of raising questions about this orientation, the mainstream media—our collective nervous system—serve to rationalize that belief system. Only a very narrow spectrum of opinion is considered acceptable, "realistic," and whatever problems arise require only a few minor adjustments here and there. As the earth begins to burn, as ecosystems start to collapse, the media focus our collective attention on the things that really matter: the Superbowl, the price of gas, the latest murder or sex scandal.

The Liberation of Collective Attention. Who owns our attention, and who should have the right to decide what happens to it? Rowe concludes that we need a new freedom movement, to "battle for the cognitive commons. If we have no choice regarding what fills our attention, then we really have no choice at all." From a Buddhist perspective, however, it seems doubtful that any social protest movement could be successful without an alternative understanding of what our attention is and what alternative practices promote more liberated attention. It is not enough to fight against billboards and Internet banner ads without also considering: what does it really mean for awareness to be here-and-now, deconditioned from attention traps both individual and collective? Is awareness to be valued as a means to some other end, or should we cherish its liberation as the most valuable end? The Buddhist answer to such questions is clear. What is less clear is what role that answer might play in our collective response to the challenge.

Healing Ecology

We are here to awaken from the illusion of our separateness.
—Thich Nhat Hanh

I came to realize clearly that mind is no other than mountains and rivers and the great wide earth, the sun and the moon and the stars.
—Dogen

What can Buddhism contribute to our understanding of the ecological crisis? As a complex religious tradition, or group of traditions, Buddhism naturally has a lot to say about the natural world. Passages in many Buddhist texts reveal sensitivity to the beauties of nature and respect for its various beings. A good example is the Jataka tales ("birth stories") that describe the previous lives of the Buddha before he became the Buddha. In many of them he is born as an animal, and in some of the best-known tales the Buddha sacrifices himself for "lower animals," such as offering his rabbit body to a weak tigress so that she can feed her starving cubs. By implication, such fables challenge the duality usually assumed between humans and "nature"—as if we were not part of nature! They suggest that the welfare of every living being, no matter how insignificant it may seem to us, is spiritually important and deserving of our concern. All beings in the Jatakas are able to feel compassion for others and act selflessly to help ease their suffering. In contrast to a Darwinian "survival of the fittest," which is often used to justify our abuse of other species, its stories offer a vision of life in which we are all interconnected, parts of the same web of life, and therefore also *inter-responsible,* responsible for each other.

This compassion is not limited to the animal realm. If we can believe the traditional biographies, the Buddha was born under trees, meditated under trees, experienced his great awakening under trees, often taught under trees, and passed away under trees. Unsurprisingly, he often expressed his gratitude to trees and other plants. Some later Buddhist texts explicitly deny that plants have sentience, but the Pali Canon is more ambiguous. In one sutra, a tree spirit appears to the Buddha in a dream, complaining that its tree had been chopped down by a monk. The next morning the Buddha prohibited Sangha members from cutting down trees. *Bhikkhu* monks and *bhikkhuni* nuns are still forbidden from cutting off tree limbs, picking flowers, even plucking green leaves off plants. What would the Buddha have to say about our wanton destruction of whole ecosystems?

Yet great sensitivity to nature is hardly unique to Buddhism. In general, the Indian traditions have identified more with the natural world than the Abrahamic traditions (Judaism, Christianity, Islam), which have emphasized the uniqueness of human beings and our dominion over the rest of creation. All these traditions teach "do not kill," but the Abrahamic commandment protects other human beings, whereas the Indian traditions stress the sanctity of all life. Nevertheless, the West has also celebrated many important counter-examples: for example, Saint Francis in the Middle Ages, more recently romantic poets and visionaries, and today environmental movements such as deep ecology. What special perspective, if any, does Buddhism offer to our understanding of the biosphere, and our relationship to it, at this critical time in history when we are doing our utmost to destroy it?

To answer that, we have to go back to a more basic question: what is really distinctive about Buddhism? The four noble (or "ennobling") truths are all about *dukkha,* and the Buddha emphasized that his only concern was ending *dukkha.* To end our *dukkha,* however, we need to understand and experience *anatta,* our lack of self, which seen from the other side is also our interdependence with all other things.

There are different ways to explain *anatta,* yet fundamentally it denies our separation from other people and, yes, from the rest of the natural world. The psycho-social construction of a separate self *in here* is at the same time the construction of an "other" *out there,* that which is different from me. What is special about the Buddhist perspective is its emphasis on the *dukkha* built into this situation. Basically, the self *is* dukkha.

One way to express the problem is that the sense of self, being a construct, is always insecure, because inherently ungrounded. It can never secure itself because there is no-*thing* that could be secured. The self is more like a process, or a function. The problem with processes, however, is that they are always temporal, necessarily impermanent—but we don't want to be impermanent, something that is changing all the time. We want to be *real!* So we keep trying to ground ourselves, often in ways that just make our situation worse. For Buddhism the only true solution lies in realizing our nonduality with "others" and understanding that our own well-being cannot be distinguished from their well-being.

That brings us to the really interesting question, ecologically. Does this basic insight about the intimate connection between sense of self and *dukkha* also apply to the sense of separation between *us* and *them*? The issue here is whether "separate self = *dukkha*" also holds true for our biggest collective sense of self: the duality between us as a species, *Homo sapiens sapiens,* and the rest of the biosphere.

Expressed in that way, the question seems rather abstract, but if this particular parallel between individual and collective selves holds, there are two important implications. First, our collective sense of separation from the natural world must also be a constant source of collective frustration for us. Secondly, our responses to that alienation, by trying to make our collective species-self more *real*—in this case, by attempting to secure or "self-ground" ourselves technologically and economically—are actually making things worse.

These are pretty big claims. What are they really pointing at? "Our species' alienation from nature is an ongoing source of collective *dukkha*"—what can that mean?

Earlier I referred to the way that the Abrahamic religions assign humans to a special place and role in creation, superior to all other creatures. Western civilization developed out of the interaction between Judeo-Christianity and the culture of classical Greece (inherited by Rome). Greece emphasized our uniqueness in a different way: by distinguishing the conventions of human society (culture, technology, etc.) from the rhythms of the natural world. What is important about this distinction is the realization that *whatever is social convention can be changed:* we can reconstruct our own societies and in that way (attempt to) determine our own collective destiny.

Today we take that insight for granted, yet it's not something that most pre-modern, traditionally conservative societies would have understood. Without our sense of historical development, they have usually accepted their own social conventions as inevitable because also *natural*. This often served to justify social arrangements that we now view as unjust, but there is nevertheless a psychological benefit in thinking that way: such societies shared a collective sense of *meaning* that we have lost today. For them, the meaning of their lives was built into the cosmos and revealed by their religion, which they took for granted. For us, in contrast, the meaning of our lives and our societies has become something that we have to determine for ourselves in a universe whose meaningfulness (if any) is no longer obvious. Even if we *choose* to be religious, we today must decide between various religious possibilities, which diminishes the spiritual security that religions have traditionally provided. While we have a freedom that pre-modern societies did not have, we lack their kind of "social security," which is the basic psychological comfort that comes from knowing one's place and role in the world.

In other words, part of the rich cultural legacy that the Greeks bequeathed the West—for better and worse—is an increasing anxiety about who we are and what it means to be human. There is a basic tension between such freedom (we decide what to value and what to do) and security (being grounded in something greater, which is taking care of us), and we want both. As soon as one of them is emphasized, we want more of the other. In general, however, the modern history of the West is a story of increasing freedom at the cost of decreasing security, in the sense that loss of faith in God has left us rudderless. Thanks to ever more powerful technologies, it seems like we can accomplish almost anything we want to do—yet we don't know what our role is, what we *should* do. That continues to be a source of great anxiety, not only for us individually but collectively. What sort of world do we want to live in? What kind of society should we have? If we can't depend on God to tell us, we are thrown back upon ourselves, and our lack of any grounding greater than ourselves is a profound source of *dukkha*.

I think that is how we can understand the first implication mentioned above: the claim that our collective sense of separation from the natural world is a continual source of frustration. The stronger our alienation from nature, the greater our anxiety. Aren't the narcissism and nihilism that have become so common today expressions of that anxiety? It's the same as our individual problem: the stronger my personal sense of alienation from other people, the more likely that I will become anxious or depressed. Recently psychologists have been realizing that, once a very basic level of food and shelter has been attained, the most important factor determining happiness is our relationships with other people. Might that also be true collectively? What does that imply about our species' estrangement from the rest of the biosphere?

We have yet to consider the second implication mentioned above, that our collective response to this collective *dukkha* is just making things worse. What does that mean?

First, let's remember how things go wrong individually. We usually respond to the delusion of a separate self by trying to make that sense of self more *real*—which doesn't work and can't work, since there is no such self that can be isolated from its relationships with others. Since we don't realize this, however, we tend to get caught up in vicious circles. I never have enough money or power, I'm never famous enough, attractive enough… Is there a collective parallel to these sorts of compulsions?

Consider our attitude toward economic growth and technological development. What motivates them? Obviously, we enjoy our comfort and wealth—but when do we have *enough*? When will our GNP be large enough? When will have all the technology we need? Perhaps we are deceived by the word "progress," because of course one can never have enough progress if it really is progress. Yet why do we think that *more* is always *better*?

When we think about our collective response from this perspective, I think the motivation becomes clear. Lacking the security that comes from knowing one's place and role in the cosmos, we have been trying to create our own security. Technology, in particular, is our collective attempt to control the conditions of our existence on this earth. We have been trying to remold the earth so that it is completely adapted to serve our purposes, until everything becomes subject to our will, a "resource" that we can use. Ironically, though, this hasn't been providing the sense of security and meaning that we seek. We have become more anxious, not less. That's because technology can be a great means but in itself it's a poor goal. Ask any dictator: once you crave power you can never have enough security to feel safe yourself.

Technology and economic growth in themselves can't resolve the basic human problem about the meaning of our lives. Since we are not sure how else to solve that problem, however, they have become a collective substitute, forms of secular salvation that we seek but never quite attain. Yet again, means have become ends. Because we don't really know where we want to go, or what we should value, we have become obsessed with control. That is why we can never have enough technological or economic development.

If the above two implications are true, something like the ecological crisis is inevitable. Sooner or later, one way or another, we will bump up against the limits of this compulsive but doomed project of endless growth. That does not mean there is no solution. It does mean that we need to understand the roots of the problem better, and find ways to address those roots more directly. Since our increasing reliance on technology as the solution to life's problems is itself a large part of the problem, the ecological crisis does not call for a primarily technological response (although technological changes are certainly necessary). Dependence on sophisticated, ever more powerful technologies tends to aggravate our sense of separation from the natural world, whereas any successful solution (if the parallel still holds) must involve accepting that we are part of the natural world. That, of course, also means embracing our responsibility for the well-being of the biosphere, because its well-being ultimately cannot be distinguished from our own well-being. Understood properly, our taking care of the earth's rainforests is like me taking care of my own leg.

So is the solution somehow "returning to nature"? We cannot return to nature because we have never left it. The environment is not really an environment. The word "environment" literally means the conditions within which a person or thing dwells. That way of describing the natural world is already dualistic, because it dichotomizes between us and where we are located. The environment is not merely the place where we live and act, for the biosphere is the ground from which and within which we arise. The earth is not only our home, it is our mother. In fact, our relationship is even more intimate, because we can never cut the umbilical cord. The air in my lungs, like the water and food that pass through my mouth, is part of a great system that does not stop with me but continually circulates through me. My life is a dissipative process that depends upon and contributes to that never-ending circulation. Eventually I too will be food for worms.

According to this understanding, our problem is not technology in itself but the obsessive ways that we have been motivated to exploit it. Without those motivations, we would be able to evaluate our technologies better, in light of the ecological problems they have contributed to, as well as the ecological solutions they might contribute to. Given all the long-term risks associated with nuclear power, for example, I cannot see that as anything but a short-sighted solution to our energy needs. In place of fossil fuels, the answer will probably be—I'm inclined to say, will *have* to be—renewable sources of power (solar, wind, etc.) along with a radically reduced need for energy. As long as we assume the necessity for continuous economic and technological expansion, the prospect of a steep reduction in our energy needs is absurd. A new understanding of our basic situation opens up other possibilities.

But wait a moment… How does any of this resolve the basic problem outlined above: the anxiety that plagues us today because we have to create our own meaning in a world where God has died? Like it or not, individual and collective self-consciousness has alienated us from pre-modern worldviews and the "natural" meaning-of-life that they provided. Nor would we want to return to such worldviews—often imposed and maintained by force—even if we could. But what other alternatives are possible? Or are we just fated to endure this existential kind of *dukkha*?

This objection helps us to see that any genuine solution to the ecological crisis must involve something more than technological improvements. Again, if the root of the problem is spiritual, the solution must also have a spiritual dimension. And again, this does not mean a return to pre-modern religious conviction, which is impossible for us today. Buddhism shows another way, which de-emphasizes the role of dogma and ritual. The Buddhist approach is quite pragmatic. The goal of the Buddhist path is wisdom in service of personal and social transformation. This, however, is quite different from the sort of rational self-reformation that Greek thinkers sought. When we meditate, for example, we are not transforming ourselves. We are being transformed. Quiet, focused concentration enables something else to work in us and through us, something other than one's usual ego-self. This opens us up and liberates a deeper grounding within ourselves. Our lack of self *(anatta)* is what enables this process.

This "something else" frees us from the compulsion to secure ourselves within the world. We do not need to become more real by becoming wealthy, or famous, or powerful, or beautiful. That is not because we identify with some other spiritual reality apart from the world. Rather, we are able to realize our nonduality with the world because we are freed from such fixations.

How does that affect the meaning of one's life? Although living beings are numberless, the bodhisattva vows to save them all. He or she assumes the grandest possible role, on a path that can never come to an end. Although such a commitment is not compulsory, it follows naturally from realizing that none of those beings is separate from oneself.

So we conclude with one final parallel between the personal and the collective. We discover the meaning we seek in the ongoing, long-term task of repairing the rupture between us and mother earth, our natural ground. That healing will transform us as much as the biosphere.

The Karma of Food

What can Buddhism teach us about genetically modified food? Needless to say, Shakyamuni and his followers didn't know anything about the genetic structure of life, much less the possibilities of modifying it technologically. It is not surprising, then, that I have not been able to find references to genetically modified (GM) organisms in any Buddhist sutra or commentary, although I admit that my search has not been very thorough. The alternative is to see whether traditional Buddhist teachings—especially (but not only) those pertaining to food practices—might give us some insight into our new situation. These may help us determine what a Buddhist should or shouldn't eat, but we also need to consider some of the larger issues that GM food raises, particularly the ways that new food technologies are being promoted.

Because of how Buddhism spread, and the diversity of Buddhist cultures that resulted, Buddhism has tended to adapt to local dietary customs, rather than import and impose food restrictions. Given the difficult climate of Tibet, for example, it is not surprising that Tibetan Buddhists have usually eaten more meat than vegetables. Another factor encouraging this variety is that, in general, Buddhism has been less concerned about what we eat than how we eat it, since our *dukkha* is rooted in our craving—and food is the second most popular example of human craving.

Nevertheless, some important distinctions within Buddhism and among Buddhists have had important implications for food practices:

especially the difference between monastics and laypeople, and the difference between Theravada (traditionally South Asian) and Mahayana (traditionally Central and East Asian) Buddhism. *Bhikkhu* monks and *bhikkhuni* nuns are expected to live a simple life largely unconcerned about mundane matters such as food. In most Buddhist societies they eat only before noon (and usually only once). According to the *Patimokha* that regulates their daily lives, "There are many fine foods such as these: ghee, butter, oil, honey, molasses, fish, meat, milk, and curds. If any *bhikkhu* who is not sick should ask for them and consume them, it is an offense entailing expiation." Notice the careful wording. Evidently the problem is not with these foods themselves, but that seeking them and indulging in them is a distraction from what monastics should be concentrating on. There is no suggestion that lay followers should also avoid them, and the careful qualification—"any *bhikkhu* who is not sick"—is a good example of the pragmatic Buddhist approach. There may be times when monastics too would benefit from consuming them.

The main food issue for Buddhists has been, and continues to be, whether one should be vegetarian. Historically, this has been somewhat complicated by the (contested) fact that, according to the earliest account we have, the *Mahaparinibbana Sutta,* Shakyamuni Buddha died of a stomach ailment apparently caused or aggravated by eating pork. Buddhist vegetarians have sometimes considered this fact scandalous and denied it, but it is consistent with what we know about the early Buddhist community.

According to the *Vinaya* rules established and followed by the Buddha himself, Theravada monastics are mendicants. They do not grow or raise their own food, they beg for it. Being dependent on what is donated to them each morning, they are not required to be vegetarian—with an important restriction often followed by devout laypeople as well: not to eat meat (or fish) if you know or have reason to suspect that it was killed *for you.* "If a *bhikkhu* sees, hears, or suspects that it has been killed for his sake, he may not eat it."

Why not? It seems a compassionate policy, given Buddhist emphasis on not harming living beings. Nevertheless, the issue of animal suffering is cited in Buddhist texts less often than the consequences for one's own karma. Even when those texts mention the importance of compassion, the main concern is often the negative effects of meat-eating on one's own capacity to cultivate compassion.

I once heard a Buddhist teacher say that it is okay to eat meat, provided that it has passed through three pairs of hands before it gets to you—as if, somehow, the karma has "worn off" by then! This seems a rather self-centered attitude, taking advantage of the unfortunate situation of others who willingly or unwillingly have the job of butchering and processing meat for the rest of us to consume. Today the mechanics of the meat industry assures us that many hands have had a role in preparing our meat, but I think that does not necessarily resolve the important issue, from a Buddhist perspective. One might conclude that none of those plastic-wrapped chickens in the supermarket has been slaughtered for me, yet one can just as well argue, given the way the food industry functions, that any I might purchase has been slaughtered for me, because all of them have been raised and killed for all of us consumers.

Today there is a movement among expatriate Tibetan Buddhists (most of whom now live in the more tropical climate of India) to become more vegetarian, led by the Dalai Lama (who nevertheless sometimes eats meat for health reasons). This development is consistent with a general Mahayana emphasis on vegetarianism, a concern especially strong in China and textually supported by well-known Mahayana scriptures such as the *Lankavatara Sutra,* the *Surangama Sutra,* and the *Brahma's Net Sutra.* These sutras claim that eating meat:

- was prohibited by the Buddha (according to the Lankavatara)
- is inconsistent with the first Buddhist precept, which prohibits taking the life of any living being
- produces bad breath and foul smells that inspire fear in other beings
- inhibits compassion and causes suffering to animals
- prevents progress in Buddhist practice and causes bad karma (e.g., you may be reborn as a lower animal), and…
- you may be eating a former relative

In accord with this, in the sixth century Chinese Buddhism (unlike Theravadan Buddhism) began to emphasize vegetarianism. Chinese and Korean monastics today continue to abstain from meat and fish (often milk products and fertilized eggs too). Curiously, it seems to have been the laity that played a leading role in this transformation. Under the influence of Mahayana sutras such as the ones mentioned above, as well as popular stories about karmic retribution, laypeople came to expect monastics to uphold higher standards of purity and renunciation. By the tenth century, vegetarianism had become a minimum standard to be followed by all monks and nuns in China. As in South Asia, monastics are dependent upon lay support, so the concerns of an increasing number of lay vegetarians could not be ignored.

The only other important dietary prohibition in Mahayana is to avoid the five "pungent odors," usually translated as garlic, onions, scallions, shallots, and leeks (sometimes chilies and other spices are added to this list). In addition to the often-objectionable smells associated with them—perhaps the main concern in a crowded monastic situation?—the *Surangama Sutra* claims that they are stimulants to anger if eaten raw and stimulate sexual desire when cooked.

Two points should be kept in mind regarding the above dietary restrictions. First, although monastics in principle have no choice, laypeople choosing to follow them make a personal decision, in the sense that such practices are not required in order to be a Buddhist or follow the Buddhist path. Not observing them may create bad karma and make one's spiritual path more difficult to follow, but that is one's own decision. Second, as mentioned earlier, often the key to Buddhist self-cultivation is less the "outer practice" of what one does than the "inner path" of how one does it. This is especially emphasized in Mahayana, which has a somewhat more relaxed attitude toward observances and regulations.

The importance of *upaya* ("skillful means") may prompt us to break precepts in some situations, yet that may be okay, because Buddhist rules, like other teachings, are pragmatic rather than absolute. Since they have not been imposed upon us by a deity, the issue is not sin or disobedience but our *dukkha* and the best way to alleviate it. A moral mistake is not an offense against God but an unskillful act that causes more trouble for ourselves as well as for others. Precepts are vows I make to myself, that I will try to live in a certain way, with the understanding that if I break them then I will bear the karmic consequences. When I fall short, then, what is appropriate is not to feel guilty but to get up, dust myself off, and try again.

To sum this up, Buddhism has generally had a flexible attitude toward most food practices, especially those of laypeople. So, to return to the topic with which we opened this chapter: what does this imply, if anything, about genetically modified food?

Let's begin with a 1996 press release by the Dharma Realm Buddhist Association, a Chinese institution with headquarters in the City of Ten Thousand Buddhas in California.

BUDDHISTS CONDEMN GENETICALLY
ENGINEERED FOODS; ADVOCATE LABELING
A major international Buddhist organization has formally condemned genetic engineering of food and advocated its

required labeling. This is the text of Dharma Realm Buddhist Association's resolution:

Genetic engineering of food is not in accord with the teachings of Buddhism. Genetic engineering of food is unwarranted tampering with the natural patterns of our world at the most basic and dangerous level.

Lack of labeling of genetically engineered food is a de facto violation of religious freedom. Without labeling, Buddhists have no way to avoid purchasing foods that violate their basic religious beliefs and principles; and Buddhist vegetarians have no way to avoid purchasing foods that contain genes from non-vegetarian sources.

All countries are urged to require labeling of all genetically engineered food.

Although I share the concern expressed in this press release about tampering with nature, there is nevertheless a problem with such an absolute claim that genetically modified food does not accord with Buddhist teachings. There is virtually no support for the position that "unnatural is bad" in any important Buddhist text, because Buddhism does not valorize nature or "being natural" in the way that the West has often done. The notion that "it's best to be natural"—a principle important in the lifestyle of many Western converts—may or may not be wise but it is not particularly Buddhist. Buddhism generally has had a non-normative understanding of nature, which does not appeal to "natural law" or some similar standard that must be observed. As Lambert Schmithausen concluded from studying ecological ethics in the early Buddhist tradition, the Pali Canon emphasizes the beauty of nature less than the struggle for life, the prevalence of greed and suffering, and most of all the universality of impermanence and decay. Our distinctively Western ambivalence between infatuation with technological progress, and romanticist nostalgia for a return-to-nature, is un-Buddhist, because Buddhism does not assume such a duality between them.

This implies that Asian Buddhists are unlikely to object to GM food because it is "unnatural." As the Dharma Realm press release suggests, however, the situation is somewhat more complicated. Perhaps the best way to unravel these complications is by referring to the discussions of two focus groups, which were conducted in Vancouver in 2004. One of the groups was composed of Theravadan lay Buddhists, all of whom agreed that, although it is important for consumers to know if food has been genetically modified and be able to choose, there is nothing in the five precepts that implies a scientist should not take a gene from one species and transfer it to another one. They said that genetic modification "is not a big problem…if it is going to improve the food" and if "it's for the whole world—the human race." Most of them would eat a tomato containing an anti-freeze fish gene, because there is "nothing in the Buddhist perspective that says the natural tomato is the right tomato." As they also pointed out, focusing on "naturalness" would be inconsistent with Buddhist emphasis on the impermanence of all things.

The Dharma Realm Buddhist Association, however, is not Theravadan but is a Chinese organization. It may be no coincidence, then, that in the Chinese Religions focus group (it's not clear how many of its members considered themselves Buddhist) one person mentioned a Buddhist friend who "has great difficulties with eating a tomato that has a fish gene in it because that violates what she is practicing. And she feels it's really wrong for that [option] not to be presented to her." The main issue for the friend seemed to be animal-to-plant gene transfer, which could be problematic for vegetarians.

One can accept that lack of labeling violates her right to have a choice, regardless of her reasons for demanding it, but from a Buddhist perspective the question still remains: *why* does a single fish gene violate her Buddhist vegetarianism? The usual Buddhist objections to consuming meat and fish—cruelty to animals, bad karma, violating the first precept, bad breath, eating a relative—can perhaps be avoided, depending upon how the genetic modification was conducted. Part of the difficulty may be due to ignorance of genetics: implanting a fish gene sounds like putting a piece of fish in the tomato. Is the problem that such a tomato is *unnatural*? For members of the Theravada Buddhist focus group, a genetically modified chicken—for example, so enlarged for breast meat that it could not walk—clearly would be unacceptable, not because such a chicken is unnatural, but because such a chicken would suffer. For the Chinese group, in contrast, transferring genes between plants was probably okay, "but where do you stop?…It's impossible to draw the line."

The simplest explanation for the difference between these concerns brings us back to the point about cultural interaction mentioned at the beginning. The members of the Theravada focus group (all from Myanmar, as it happened) are more consistent with the earliest teachings, which do not privilege "the natural." In contrast, Chinese Buddhism has naturally (!) been somewhat influenced by traditional cultural values that emphasize harmony within society (Confucianism) and with nature (Taoism). This, of course, does not make Chinese Buddhism any less authentic as a type of Buddhism, yet it is important not to conflate it with Theravada Buddhism. Can we conclude that from a Chinese Buddhist perspective no genetically modified food should be consumed, because it's unnatural? We are reminded that there is no *Buddhism,* only *Buddhisms.* So: Where do those differences leave us?

The Cetana *of GM Food.* Both the Theravada and Chinese focus groups expressed concern about the motivations behind the introduction of genetic modifications into food. According to a Chinese member, "it's not just about scientific capability but whether we *should* do it." In explaining why we should not eat animals that have been slaughtered for us, Theravada participants highlighted the importance of *cetana,* "intentional action" in Buddhist teachings. This emphasis on motivation and intention points at what is distinctive about the Buddhist perspective, but what does that specifically imply for genetically modified food? We need to go beyond the issue of traditional dietary restrictions—as we have seen, not such a major issue for Buddhism—to consider broader issues about how consistent GM food is with Buddhism's basic worldview and understanding of human motivation. What role is the introduction of GM food likely to play, if any, in our individual and collective struggles with *dukkha*?

The Buddhist understanding of karma as *cetana* has been discussed in earlier chapters, and so have the three unwholesome roots (the three poisons). Here, however, it is helpful to remember what are usually called the three "basic facts": *dukkha* ("dis-ease"), *anicca* ("impermanence"), and *anatta* ("not-self"). We have seen that Buddhism has a rather subtle understanding of what makes us unhappy—more precisely, of how we make ourselves unhappy. It is intimately related to the other two basic teachings, impermanence and nonself.

Anicca means that nothing is eternal, everything arising and passing away according to conditions, including ourselves. Socially, this implies an openness to change, including progress—if it really is progress, that is, an improvement of previous conditions. New technologies are not in themselves a problem, for the important issue is their effects on our *dukkha*. Buddhism is not nostalgic for some prelapsarian time when life was "natural," because there never was such a golden age.

In contrast, *anatta*, "not-self", involves realizing that nothing has any "self-essence," not only because there is no permanence, but also because everything is interdependent on everything else, part of a web so tightly woven that each phenomenon in the universe is both effect and cause of all other phenomena. This "interpermeation" is well expressed by Thich Nhat Hanh, in a famous passage from *The Heart of Understanding* that every Buddhist should be familiar with:

> If you are a poet, you will see clearly that there is a cloud floating in this sheet of paper. Without a cloud, there will be no rain; without rain, the trees cannot grow, and without trees we cannot make paper. The cloud is essential for the paper to exist. If the cloud is not here, the sheet of paper cannot be here either....
>
> If we look into this sheet of paper even more deeply, we can see the sunshine in it. If the sunshine is not there, the tree cannot grow. In fact, nothing can grow. Even we cannot grow without sunshine. And so, we know that the sunshine is also in this sheet of paper. The paper and the sunshine *inter-are.* And if we continue to look, we can see the logger who cut the tree and brought it to the mill to be transformed into paper. And we see the wheat. We know that the logger cannot exist without his daily bread, and therefore the wheat that became his bread is also in this sheet of paper. And the logger's father and mother are in it too....
>
> You cannot point out one thing that is not here—time, space, the earth, the rain, the minerals in the soil, the sunshine, the cloud, the river, the heat. Everything co-exists with this sheet of paper....As thin as this sheet of paper is, it contains everything in the universe in it.

Notice that this way of deconstructing "separate-thing-ness" (*svabhava,* literally "self-being") does not discriminate between natural phenomena (sun, rain, trees) and more technological ones (e.g., the chainsaw that the logger uses, or the paper mill that processes the wood pulp). In short, nothing has any reality of its own, because nothing *is* on its own. Everything is part of everything else.

If we don't need to worry about disturbing genetic "essences," doesn't that liberate us to do whatever we want technologically? Not quite, because the most important criterion for Buddhism remains *dukkha*. Does a genetic modification tend to reduce that, or increase it?

For a brief period, "golden rice" genetically engineered to include beta-carotene (which our bodies convert into vitamin A) was proposed for nutritional deficiencies in some undeveloped countries, until it was realized that the amount of beta-carotene that could be added was too small to be significant. A more important and notorious example of GM, however, was Monsanto's attempt to introduce a patented "terminator gene" into the world's main food crops, which it gave up only because of very damaging publicity. In general, the genetic modifications I have read about seem designed more for the convenience of the food industry than for the benefit of the food consumer. The focus is on growing and processing food more efficiently, rather than on taste or nutrition. In such a competitive industry, corporate convenience may end up reducing consumer prices, yet it is not otherwise clear how GM in food is actually working to reduce consumer dukkha.

On the other side, unexpected problems have repeatedly occurred, usually for those who have not asked for GM food and perhaps have little to gain from it. Monarch caterpillars feed exclusively on milkweed leaves, but in 1998 it was claimed that milkweed contamination from Bt-corn pollen (genetically altered to express the bacterial toxin Bt, which is poisonous to insects) was killing them. Also in 1998, Arpad Pusztai, a scientist working in Britain, reported that in his experiments genetically modified potatoes were causing immune system damage to rats. In 2000, StarLink corn, with a protein indigestible to humans, was accidentally released into the human food chain, leading to 37 reports of serious allergic reactions investigated by the U.S. Food and Drug Administration. In 2001, Ignacio Chapela and David Quist, researchers from the University of California, claimed to have discovered that genes from biotech corn had contaminated native maize in the Mexican highlands.

One more incident, less notorious than these others, is worth noticing. In May 2000 Monsanto revealed some amazing new information about its Roundup Ready GM soybeans. Four years after they began to be consumed, the corporation told the USDA that it had just discovered two "unexpected" DNA fragments in its genome, one 250 base-pairs in length, the other 72 base-pairs, which had somehow been unintentionally inserted, or else had been there all along, without the company's knowledge.

There are at least two reasons to be concerned about these incidents, in addition to the specific problems (allergic reactions, immune system damage, etc.) they reveal. First, they suggest what Buddhist emphasis on interdependence also implies: that meddling with the genome of food plants (and no doubt that of animals as well) is an extraordinarily complicated process with many types of subtle consequences that are very difficult to anticipate and evaluate exhaustively. In other words, we can expect these types of accidents to recur indefinitely. Second, equally disturbing has been the reaction of the food industry, which has tried to deny or minimize these incidents, and—particularly in the cases of Pusztai, and Chapela and Quist—has undertaken questionable public relations campaigns to impugn their scientific competence and personal integrity.

What do these concerns reveal about institutional motivation? We are reminded that the food industry is a food *industry*. Inevitably, then, providing nutritious and healthy food is not the ultimate *goal* in this system but the *means* within a larger economic process in which the focus, naturally, is efficiency and profitability. For our economic system food is another commodity. Genetic modification does not make food into a commodity—it is already a commodity—but the safety problems with GM food make us more aware of the problems with commodifying food, because producing safe and nutritious food appears to be more complicated than providing most other consumer products.

Given the extraordinary difficulties with testing for possible adverse effects, along with corporate pressures for short-term profitability and growth, can the food industry be trusted to subordinate its own interests in GM and place top priority on safeguarding the needs, not only of human consumers, but of the whole ecosystem? Furthermore, given strong corporate influence on the U.S. Food and Drug Administration, can the FDA today be trusted to always give top priority to the needs of consumers and the biosphere? In other words, are these yet more examples of *institutionalized greed*?

And of *institutionalized delusion*? If there is a problematical duality between the institutional interests of food producers and individual interests of consumers, there is a much greater one between the human species and the rest of the biosphere. Since the advent of the modern era, our escalating technological powers have been used to subdue and exploit the rest of the biosphere, with little concern for the consequences of our domination for other species. We continue to act as if we have no responsibility for the other beings with which we share the earth, as if they have no value or meaning except insofar as they serve our purposes. From a more nondual perspective, the ecological crisis is not a result of unanticipated "side effects." There are no side-effects, only consequences we like and those that we don't. Since we are part of the natural world, if we make nature sick, we become sick. If the biosphere dies, we die. That is as good an example of karma as we will find.

What does this imply about the karma of GM food? The genetic modification of food is only a small part of the larger commodification process, but a significant part of it, since technological modification of other plant and animal species, without a much better understanding of their genomes and how all the genomes of living creatures affect each other, is an especially dangerous example of how our ambitions tend to outrun our wisdom. To sum up, I believe that all this implies that genetic engineering of food, as presently practiced, is probably incompatible with basic Buddhist teachings, because it seems to be inconsistent with the kinds of personal and collective transformation of motivations necessary if *dukkha*—not only human *dukkha* but that of other living beings too—is to be reduced.

This does not necessarily mean that the genetic modification of food is always a bad thing to be avoided, a stance which might itself be inconsistent with the primary Buddhist emphasis on reducing *dukkha*. Since Buddhism does not privilege "the natural," including the natural selection that drives the evolutionary process, there is the possibility that in the future some modifications might actually serve to reduce *dukkha*. Although it would need to be very carefully tested, there is the possibility that a vitamin A–enriched rice might someday be a benefit to humankind without being a threat to the rest of the biosphere.

From a Buddhist point of view, technologies are neither good nor bad in themselves. Nor are they neutral. That is because technologies cannot be separated from the larger social, economic, and ecological contexts within which they are devised and applied. This means that any attempt at evaluating a technology such as the genetic modification of food needs to take the intentions behind those innovations into account. The Buddhist understanding of karma as *cetana* implies that, institutionally as well as individually, we can expect self-centered motivations to create more problems than they solve.

Why We Love War

In war, there are no unwounded soldiers.
—José Narosky

War is hell, and today more than ever. Although high-tech weapons make it a videogame for some, those same weapons make it unbelievably destructive for many more. Whatever valor was once associated with hand-to-hand combat has long since disappeared due to gunpowder, and the massive slaughters of the twentieth century have made it increasingly difficult to romanticize the death and misery war causes. Nonetheless it continues and we have learned, if not to accept it, to take it for granted. Obviously, not everyone loathes it. The U.S. economy would collapse without the obscene amount spent on the military-industrial complex, now well over $600 billion a year according to some calculations. It's hard to rationalize such a sum without a war once in a while. That's why the end of the Cold War with the Soviet Union was so disconcerting. What would we do without an enemy! Fortunately the war on terror fits the bill perfectly. With a bit of luck it may never end (how would we know?) and the military budget can balloon forever.

But it's not only those who get rich (or richer) off war who like it. They couldn't promote war if the rest of us weren't willing to go along with their manipulations. We support and follow the war-makers because, to tell the truth, there is something in us that finds war agreeable...even attractive. Can Buddhism help us understand what that is?

The official excuse for every war is always the same: self-defense. It's okay to kill other people and destroy their society because that's what they want to do to us. As Hermann Goering said, "The people can always be brought to the bidding of the leaders....Just tell them they are being attacked, and denounce the peacemakers for lack of patriotism and exposing the country to danger." They haven't attacked us yet? Then we need a "preventive war." That suggests the problem with all "just war" theories. Once there's such a thing as a just war, every war becomes marketed as a just war.

But that's not why we like war. That's just how the propaganda works, how leaders get us to line up behind them. What makes us so gullible? Why are we so willing to sacrifice ourselves, even our children? Why doesn't exposing the lies of the last war inoculate us against the deceptions that will be used to promote the next one?

Buddhist societies have not been immune from war. The Japanese Buddhist establishment wholeheartedly supported the imperialist ambitions of its fascist government. In Sri Lanka today politicized Buddhist monks oppose a negotiated solution to a civil war that has already cost thousands of lives. In all the cases that I can think of, however, people who consider themselves Buddhists became belligerent because their Buddhism had become mixed up with a more secular religion: nationalism. Such war-mongering startles us because it so obviously contradicts Buddhist principles—not only incompatible with its emphasis on not harming, but also inconsistent with a worldview that emphasizes wisdom over power.

From a Buddhist perspective, the various conflicts in the Middle East look like a family quarrel. That's because the three Abrahamic faiths—Judaism, Christianity, and Islam—share much the same understanding of the world. It's a feud among brothers who have fallen out, which is, of course, sometimes the most vicious sort. Having been raised by the same father, they have a similar worldview: this world is a battleground where the good must fight against those who are evil. The most important issue is where each of us stands in this cosmic struggle. Our salvation depends upon it. It's necessary to choose sides.

It is not surprising, then, that the al-Qaeda understanding of good and evil—the need for a holy war against evil—is also shared by the administration of George W. Bush. Bin Laden would no doubt agree with what Bush has emphasized: "If you're not with us, you're against us." Since there is no room in this grand cosmic struggle for neutrality, neither of them is much concerned about the fate of innocent bystanders. Bystanders are not innocent. Once something has been labeled as evil, the focus must be on fighting it. The most important thing is to do whatever is necessary to destroy it. This implies a preoccupation with power and victory at any cost. Whether one supports small-group terrorism or state terrorism, the issue is the same. Which will be more powerful, the forces of good or the forces of evil?

Buddhism offers a different perspective. In place of this battle-ground of wills where good contends against evil, the most impor-tant struggle is a spiritual one between ignorance and delusion, on the one side, and liberating wisdom on the other. And seeing the world primarily as a war between good and evil is one of our more dangerous delusions.

Looking back over history, we can see that when leaders have tried to destroy evil, they have usually ended up creating more evil. An obvious example is the heresy inquisitions and witch-trials of medieval Europe, but for sheer violence and *dukkha* nothing can match the persecutions of the twentieth century. What was Adolf Hitler trying to do with his "final solution" to the "Jewish prob-lem"? The earth could be made pure for the Aryan race only by exterminating the Jews, along with all the other vermin (gypsies, homosexuals, the mentally defective, etc.) who contaminate it. Stalin killed well-to-do Russian peasants because he was trying to create his ideal society of collective farmers. Mao Zedong eliminated Chinese landlords for the same reason. Like Bush and bin Laden, they were trying to perfect the world by eliminating its evil people. So one of the main causes of evil in our world has been attempts to get rid of evil (or what has been seen as evil). In more Buddhist terms, much of the world's suffering has resulted from this delusive way of thinking about good and evil.

For Buddhism, however, this simplistic way of understanding conflict keeps us from looking deeper and finding other ways to resolve differences. What we call evil is, like everything else, an effect of causes and conditions, and it's important to realize what those causes are. Buddhism emphasizes evil itself less than the three *roots* of evil (also known as the three unwholesome roots, or the three poisons): greed, ill will, and delusion. The Buddhist solution to suffering does not involve answering violence with violence, any more than it involves responding to greed with greed, or responding to delusion with more delusion. As the most famous verse in the Dhammapada says, hatred *(vera)* is never appeased by hatred; it is appeased by non-hatred *(avera)*. We must look for ways to break that cycle by transmuting those poisons into their positive counterparts: greed into generosity, ill will into loving-kindness, and delusion into wisdom.

The Buddhist path involves understanding how our minds work, and Buddhist teachers warn us about how our minds get stuck in dualistic ways of thinking: not only good and evil, but success and failure, rich and poor, and so forth. We often distinguish between such terms because we want one side rather than the other, yet we cannot have one without the other, because the meaning of each depends upon (negating) the other. They are two sides of the same coin. If, for example, it is important for me to live a pure life (whatever that may mean to me), that doesn't mean I escape impurity. On the contrary, I have to think about impurity all the time: I will be preoccupied with (avoiding) impurity. We cannot have one side without the other, and together they distort the world for us. We do not experience the world as it is, but as filtered through such ways of thinking. As Chan master Huihai put it, true purity is a state beyond purity and impurity. By getting caught up in such dualisms, we "bind ourselves without a rope."

What does this mean for the duality of good versus evil? It's the same trap. We don't know what is good until we know what is evil, and we can't feel that we are good unless we are fighting against that evil. We can feel comfortable and secure in our own goodness *inside* only by attacking some evil *outside* us. There is something quite satisfying about this struggle between good (us) and evil (them), because it makes sense of the world. Think of the plot of every James Bond film, every Star Wars film, every Indiana Jones film, every Harry Potter book and movie, and so forth—you can add your own favorites to this list. The bad guys are stereotypes because they play a pre-determined role in our collective fantasy. Being ruthless, without remorse, they must be stopped by any means necessary. We are meant to feel that it is okay (and, to tell the truth, it's quite enjoyable) to see them get beaten up. Because the villains like to hurt people, it's all right to hurt them. Because they like to kill people, it's okay to kill them.

While such stories entertain us, they reinforce this worldview. What do they teach us? That if you want to hurt someone, it's important to demonize them first, to fit them into a good-versus-evil story by labeling *them* as evil. Even school bullies usually begin by looking for some petty offense that they can use to justify their own penchant for violence. That is also why the first casualty of war is truth. The media must sell some such story to the people: "In order to defend ourselves, we must…"

Does that get at why we like war? Wars cut through the petty problems of daily life, and unite us good guys here against the bad guys there. There is fear in that, of course, yet there's also something exhilarating about it. The meaning of life becomes simpler and clearer in wartime. As Chris Hedges explains it in his first-hand account of life as a war correspondent, *War Is a Force That Gives Us Meaning:* "The communal march against an enemy generates a warm, unfamiliar bond with our neighbors, our community, our nation, wiping out unsettling undercurrents of alienation and dislocation. War, in times of malaise and desperation, is a potent distraction." The problems with my life, and yours, are not personal anymore but *over there*—the enemy that is trying to kill us. That makes the solution simple—we must get them first.

Such ways of thinking and feeling are dangerous. Nevertheless, understanding good-versus-evil as a dualism that deludes us is not by itself sufficient for understanding the enduring attraction of war. That dualism rationalizes a more basic reason why war is so addictive. Let's look again at our susceptibility to its "potent distraction." Something else that Hedges says is quite suggestive:

> The enduring attraction of war is this: even with its destruction and carnage it can give us what we long for in life. It can give us purpose, meaning, a reason for living. Only when we are in the midst of conflict does the shallowness and vapidness of much of our lives become apparent. Trivia dominates our conversations and increasingly our airwaves....[War] allows us to be noble.

The title of Hedges' book makes a critically important point: war gives meaning to our lives. This gives us insight into the psychology of terrorism. Why would someone want to crash hijacked airplanes into skyscrapers, killing thousands—including oneself—and terrorizing millions? Perhaps only religion can provide the motivation and collective support for such terrible deeds, because religion, ironically, is what usually teaches us the ultimate meaning of life. Mark Juergensmeyer's study of religious terrorism, *Terror in the Mind of God,* clarifies the connection: "A society provides an accepted—even heroic—social role for its citizens who participate in great struggles and have been given moral license to kill. They are soldiers. Understandably, many members of radical religious movements see themselves that way."

Chris Hedges, like many other correspondents, found it difficult to return to a peaceful environment, because he had become addicted to the excitement of war. But what if there is a grand spiritual war that is going on all the time? In that case, the "vapidness" of everyday life may be avoided indefinitely.

According to Juergensmeyer:

> Such soldiers have found new battles: the grand spiritual and political struggles in which their movements envision themselves to be engaged. These cosmic wars impart a sense of importance and destiny to men who find the modern world to be stifling, chaotic, and dangerously out of control. The imagined wars identify the enemy, the imputed source of their personal and political failures; they exonerate these would-be soldiers from any responsibility for failures by casting them as victims; they give them a sense of their own potential for power; and they arm them with the moral justification, the social support, and the military equipment to engage in battle both figuratively and literally.

Such spiritual struggles can provide a heroic identity that transcends even death, for death is not checkmate when you are an agent of God. What grander destiny is possible than to be part of the cosmic forces of Good fighting against Evil? A heady alternative to languishing in a refugee camp without much hope for the future—or, for that matter, to channel-surfing and shopping at the mall. One's own death as a martyr (literally, "witness") becomes a sacrifice (literally, "making holy") that ennobles one's victims as well as oneself. All is justified because the meaning of that spiritual struggle transcends this world and its inhabitants. Juergensmeyer concludes that the modern world as experienced by religious terrorists and their supporters is

> a dangerous, chaotic, and violent sea for which religion was an anchor in a harbor of calm. At some deep and almost transcendent level of consciousness, they sensed their lives slipping out of control, and they felt both responsible for the disarray and a victim of it. To be abandoned by religion in such a world would mean a loss of their own individual identity. In fashioning a "traditional religion" of their own, they exposed their concerns not so much with their religious, ethnic or national communities as with their own personal, imperiled selves.

If the worldview, meaning, and power provided by warfare are addictive for many, what happens when military struggles are elevated into a Cosmic War between Good and Evil? The attraction of warrior-identity becomes even greater.

In short, religious terrorism helps us understand that the problem with a good-versus-evil worldview is not merely that it is a simple and comfortable way to understand the world. What did Hedges say about "the shallowness and vapidness of much of our lives"? Those words point to what is lacking in daily life for many of us. Despite its horrors, war fills the void—the shallowness, loneliness, alienation, and malaise—of everyday existence. Is this because it conceals better something that is missing in our everyday identities? Is this lack of meaning a general description of all peacetime life, which suggests a grim prognosis indeed, or does it describe the sense of lack in modern society, which seems to doom our lives to triviality insofar as it provides us with no cosmic role greater than consumerism or (occasionally) patriotism? In other words, is there something unsatisfactory and ultimately frustrating about the secular alternative that makes religious wars so attractive?

In *The Battle for God,* Karen Armstrong describes the history of fundamentalism as an attempt to fill the empty core of a society based on scientific rationalism. "Confronted with the genocidal horrors of our century, reason has nothing to say. Hence, there is a void at the heart of modern culture, which Western people experienced at an early stage of their scientific revolution"—or *began* to experience. The void is still there; we have just gotten used to avoiding or repressing the great anxiety associated with modernity, and not noticing the consequences. Armstrong reminds us of Nietzsche's madman, who declared that the death of God has torn humanity from its roots and cast us adrift "as if through an infinite nothingness," ensuring that "profound terror, a sense of meaningless and annihilation, would be part of the modern experience." Today politicians and economists urge us to keep the (secular) faith, keep telling us that we are approaching the promised land of peace and prosperity for all, but "at the end of the twentieth century, the liberal myth that humanity is progressing to an ever more enlightened and tolerant state looks as fantastic as any of the other millennial myths [that Armstrong's book examines]." The nameless dread still haunts us. Fundamentalists and secularists seem to be "trapped in an escalating spiral of hostility and recrimination." And the stakes, after 9/11, have become much higher.

According to Juergensmeyer, common to all violent religious movements is their rejection of secularism. Although the secularity of modern life is a hard-won historical legacy that has been essential for the freedoms we enjoy today, they have a point. The basic problem that they share—and that we share with them—is not the threat posed by other religions but *the ideology that pretends not to be an ideology*. The difficulty with our usual understanding of secularity is that it is an ideology that pretends to be the everyday world we live in. Many of us assume that it is simply the way the world really is, once superstitious beliefs about it have been removed. Yet that is the secular view of secularity, which needs to be questioned in order to realize how unique and peculiar such a worldview is—and ultimately how unsatisfactory.

What we tend to forget is that the distinction between sacred and secular was originally a religious distinction, meant to empower a new type of Protestant spirituality—that is, a more personal way to address our sense of *lack*. By privatizing an unmediated relationship between more individualized Christians and a more transcendent God, Martin Luther's emphasis on salvation-by-faith-alone worked to eliminate the spiritual aspects of *this* world. The medieval understanding of a continuity between the natural and the supernatural was broken by *internalizing* faith and *projecting* God's sacred realm far above this one. The newly liberated space between them created something new: the secular. As the modern world has evolved, the spiritual aspects of life have become less important while the secular has gradually become more dynamic. As the sacred pole has faded away, or become merely subjective and private, little remains visible except the secular by itself, without any spiritual perspective or moral authority.

What may be misleading about this explanation of a diminished spiritual dimension is that it still seems to suggest *superimposing* something (for example, some particular religious understanding of the meaning of our lives) onto the secular world (that is, the world "as it really is"). My point is just the opposite. Our usual understanding of the secular is a deficient *worldview* (in Buddhist terms, a delusion) distorted by the fact that one half of the original duality has gone missing, although now it has been absent so long that we have largely forgotten about it.

Why is that deficiency a problem? Because the secular world lacks something important: a valid way to understand and resolve our sense of lack, which is the basic spiritual problem. For Buddhism, this sense of lack—the feeling of something missing, that something is wrong with my life—is the shadow side of one's delusive sense of self. My sense of self, being a psychological and social construct, is by definition ungrounded and therefore intrinsically insecure. Traditional religions acknowledge this problem by explaining what the problem is (sin, for example) and what to do about it (confession, penance, and so forth). Secular modernity can only explain any sense of lack we may feel as a result of social maladjustment or some form of oppression (class, race, gender, etc.). There are many unjust social arrangements that need to be addressed, to be sure, but resolving them will not fill up the bottomless hole at one's core.

· Obsessed with an emptiness that our rationality cannot understand and does not recognize, we now try to become more real by exploiting the possibilities that the secular world offers. Individually, we have become obsessed with the symbolisms of money, status, and power. Collectively, our *lack* empowers transnational corporations that are never big or profitable enough, nation-states that are never secure enough, and accelerating technological innovation that is never innovative enough to satisfy us for very long.

To sum up, we cannot understand our secularized world without also acknowledging the sense of lack—and therefore the persistent identity-crisis—which haunts the people who live in that world. That brings us back to what Buddhism has to say about samsara, literally "going round and round." Samsara is the way this world is experienced due to our greed, ill will, and delusion, which makes it a realm of suffering. Technological development gives us opportunities to reduce many types of suffering, but for Buddhism our deepest and most problematic anxiety is due to the sense of *lack* that shadows a deluded sense-of-self. A secularized world can actually be more samsaric and addictive for us than a pre-modern one, because it is more haunted by the modern loss of traditional securities. The Buddhist solution is to undo the habitual thought-patterns and behavior-patterns that cause us to experience the world in such a diminished way, so we can realize the spiritual dimension of every-day life that has always been there—even when we have been unable to see it, due to our delusions and cravings.

In a way, I am arguing that religious fundamentalists are right, after all. The modern world can keep many of us alive longer and some-times makes death less physically painful, but it has no answer to the groundlessness that plagues us individually and collectively, for noth-ing *in* the world can fill up the bottomless hole at our core. Without understanding what motivates us, we end up clinging—not only to physical objects but also to symbols and ideologies, which tend to be the most troublesome.

That brings us back to war. If our modern, secularized world is plagued by an unacknowledged and therefore misunderstood sense of lack, it is not surprising that war too continues to be so attractive, even addictive. War can give us the meaning we crave, because it provides a reassuring way to understand what is wrong with our lives. War offers a simple way to bind together our individual lacks and project them outside, onto the enemy. *They* are evil because they want to hurt *us*. Since we are merely defending ourselves, we can feel good about what we do to them. The karma that results is not dif-ficult to understand: the cause of each war is usually the previous one.

If war is a collective response to our collective problem with lack, we cannot expect war to cease until we find better ways to address that basic spiritual problem.

Notes for a Buddhist Revolution

Buddhism is a personal path of spiritual transformation, not a program for political or economic revolution. Is it always clear, however, where the one ends and the other begins? Or is this another duality of the sort that Buddhism likes to critique/deconstruct? Together, our ways of thinking and acting create society, but the opposite is also true: social institutions condition how we think and what we do. This means that, sooner or later, the bodhisattva's concern to end *dukkha* and devotion to the awakening of everyone will bump up against the constraints of present economic and political systems, which in order to thrive need our complicity as consumers and defenders of that way of life.

According to a few scholars (most notably Trevor Ling in *The Buddha*), Shakyamuni saw the Sangha as modeling a new kind of society. Such a claim is difficult to evaluate, because almost everything we know about the Buddha was filtered through the memory of many generations of monastics before being written down. The Dharma that they eventually recorded emphasizes the differences between the life of a householder and the way of religious renunciation. Nevertheless, the Buddha's teachings still have many implications that extend beyond the individual spiritual path. He had much to say about the role of a good householder and the responsibilities of a wise ruler. As Buddhism also emphasizes, however, times change. We live in a world radically different from anything that even Shakyamuni could have anticipated, which requires creative ways of adapting his profound insights to new challenges. The greatest of those challenges, of course, is survival: not only the effects of rapid climate change on human civilization but also the continuation of countless other species threatened by our technologies and population growth. The first precept—not to harm any living being—calls upon us to consider the consequences of our actions for the biosphere as a whole.

Of course, this does not mean we can ignore the social problems that also confront us. As we know, and as Buddhism also implies, ecological, political, and economic crises are interconnected. We won't be able to meet the challenge of global warming unless we also figure out how to rein in an economic system that depends on continuous expansion if it is to avoid collapse. The fundamental issue isn't our reliance on fossil fuels but our reliance on a mindset that takes the globalization of corporate capitalism (and its dominant role in supposedly democratic processes) as natural, necessary, and inevitable. We need an alternative to "there is no alternative."

Previous chapters have offered Buddhist perspectives on institutionalized greed (consumerism and corporatism), institutionalized ill will (militarism), and institutionalized delusion (media and propaganda); the fragmentation, commodification, and manipulation of our attention; our collective addictions to war and technological dominion over the planet. We have seen how these various problems cause *dukkha*. The more difficult question is what Buddhism can contribute to solving them.

Insofar as the issue is institutionalized greed, ill will, and delusion, we can envision a more "dharmic" society whose institutions encourage generosity and compassion, grounded in a wisdom that realizes our interconnectedness. That is obvious enough but it doesn't help us very much. Is a reformed capitalism consistent with a dharmic society, or do we need altogether different kinds of economic institutions? How can our world de-militarize? Should representative democracy be revitalized by stricter controls on campaigns and lobbying, or do we need a more participatory and decentralized political system? Should newspapers and television networks be better regulated or non-profit? What should be done about advertising, which continues to colonize our collective consciousness? Can the United Nations be transformed into the kind of international organization the world needs, or does an emerging global community call for something different?

I do not think that Buddhism has the answers to these questions. We should hesitate before deriving any particular economic or political system from its various teachings. Different aspects of the Dharma can be used to support capitalism, socialism, anarchism, and (a favorite of mine) Georgism, a social and economic philosophy popularized by Henry George at the end of the nineteenth century. The basic limitation of all such arguments is that Buddhism is really about awakening and liberating our awareness, rather than prescribing new institutional structures for that awareness. We cannot pre-determine what awakened awareness should or will decide when applied to the problem of social *dukkha*. There is no magic formula to be invoked. That no one else has such a formula either, so far as I can see, means that solutions to our collective *dukkha* cannot be derived from any ideology. They must be worked out together.

This is a challenging task yet not an insuperable one, if men and women of good will can find ways to work together, without the deformations of pressure groups defending special privileges. Needless to say, that is not an easy condition to achieve, and it brings us back us to the priority of personal practice, which works to develop men and women of good will. This also suggests the role of socially engaged Buddhism: not to form a new movement but, along with other forms of engaged spirituality, to add a valuable dimension to existing movements already working for peace, social justice, and ecological responsibility.

So: what does Buddhism have to offer those movements?

The Importance of a Spiritual Practice. Buddhism begins with individual transformation. The basis of Buddhist social engagement is the necessity to work on oneself as well as on the social system. Why have so many revolutions and reform movements ended up merely replacing one gang of thugs with another? If we have not begun to transform our own greed, ill-will, and delusion, our efforts to address their institutionalized forms are likely to be useless, or worse. Even if our revolution is successful, we will merely replace one group of egos with our own. If I do not struggle with the greed inside myself, it is quite likely that, when I gain power, I too will be inclined to take advantage of the situation to serve my own interests. If I do not acknowledge the ill will in my own heart as my own problem, I am likely to project my anger onto those who obstruct my purposes. If unaware that my own sense of duality is a dangerous delusion, I will understand the problem of social change as the need for me to dominate the socio-political order. Add a conviction of my good intentions, along with my superior understanding of the situation, and one has a recipe for social as well as personal disaster. History is littered with examples.

This emphasis on one's own transformation is especially important for more individual and life-style issues such as racism, patriarchy, homophobia, "money-theism" and consumerism, and family size (i.e., how many children to have in an over-crowded world). While new laws addressing these concerns are sometimes needed, the main battle for social acceptance is fought in local communities and the most valuable tool is personal example, including the determination to make one's own attitudes apparent to others in situations that may be uncomfortable. Any solution to consumerism, for instance, must include personal demonstration of a simpler but improved quality of life based on relationships rather than consumption. Some recent economic studies have discovered that, once a minimum standard of living has been achieved (about

$10,000 per person), an increase in income has little if any effect on one's happiness. The Buddha would not be surprised.

Commitment to Nonviolence. A nonviolent approach is implied by our nonduality with "others," including those we may be struggling against. Means and ends cannot be separated. Peace is not only the goal, it must also be the way. We ourselves must be the peace we want to create. A spiritual awakening reduces our sense of separation from those who have power over us. Gandhi, for example, always treated the British authorities in India with respect. He never tried to dehumanize them, which is one reason why he was successful.

This, however, is not an argument for absolute pacifism, which seems to me a dogmatic attitude inconsistent with Buddhist pragmatism. Although one might decide to "resist not evil," I do not see that being a Buddhist is always incompatible with genuine self-defense. If my wife and son are about to be physically attacked, I have a responsibility to defend them, by force if necessary. Even in such dangerous situations, however, non-violence is usually the more appropriate and effective way to respond.

The basic problem, of course, is that once a principle of collective self-defense is accepted then every act of aggression becomes rationalized as self-defense—the 2003 invasion of Iraq being an especially ridiculous example. The solution, I suggest, is not to assert unconditional pacifism in every possible situation but to be prepared to challenge the propaganda and manipulations of those who are willing to use violence in pursuit of what they see as economic and political gain. This is a difficult issue, however, and we can expect a diversity of opinion among engaged Buddhists, because the best approach cannot be determined simply by invoking some simple dharmic principle that trumps all other considerations. We are reminded of the central importance of *upaya,* "skillful means."

Although nonviolence may not make a social struggle easier or more successful, it incorporates an essential principle: not merely wresting power from others who are misusing it but challenging their delusions in ways that might prompt them to rethink what they think they know. The righteous anger that often incites resistance movements is understandable, to say the least, yet from a Buddhist perspective it's still a form of hatred, and hatred is never a skillful response. According to one Tibetan metaphor, wanting to hurt someone is like picking up a burning coal in one's bare hand in order to throw it at someone else.

In deciding how to respond to such situations, it is important to remember that Buddhism traces our collective *dukkha* back to delusion, not to evil. The world is not a battleground where people who are good must destroy those who are evil, but the place where we do stupid things to ourselves and to each other because we are ignorant of our true nature. The fundamental social problem is that our individual and collective awareness gets manipulated in ways that aggravate rather than relieve *dukkha*. We are all victims of such manipulations, which have become institutionalized and taken on a life of their own. Our leaders or rulers have been so preoccupied with gaining and wielding power that they don't realize what their lust for power has done to themselves. Sympathy for their plight must not deflect us from working to achieve justice for their victims, but Buddhism is not concerned with one side to the exclusion of the other. Bodhisattvas vow to help *everyone* awaken.

Awakening Together. Contrary to the way that the bodhisattva path is often understood, Buddhist social engagement is not about deferring our own happiness to help others who are less fortunate because they happen to be suffering. That just reinforces a self-defeating (and self-exhausting) dualism between us and them. Rather, we join together to improve the situation for all of us. As a Native American woman put it: "If you have come here to help me, you are wasting your time. But if you have come because your liberation is tied up with mine, then let us work together." The point of the bodhisattva path is that none of us can be fully awakened until everyone "else" is too. If we are not really separate from each other, our destinies cannot really be separated from each other, either. The difficult world situation today means that sometimes bodhisattvas need to manifest their compassion in more politically engaged ways.

The six *paramitas* (perfections) that bodhisattvas develop include *kshanti* (patience) and *virya* (persistence). These are essential for self-less social action. We don't expect to be rewarded for what we do or gratified by what we've achieved. We should not expect to see the fruits of our labors, but neither are we free to give up the work. Although this can be frustrating, it accords with Buddhist emphasis on nonattachment and *tathata,* "just this!" This moment is not to be sacrificed for a future one—for example, some social utopia that may or may not be just around the corner. What is happening right here and now is whole and complete in itself, even as we devote ourselves to addressing its *dukkha.* That is the daily practice of a bodhisattva. Such an attitude, along with emphasis on one's personal spiritual practice, is the key to avoiding the exhaustion and burnout that plagues social activists.

Impermanence and Emptiness. These two Buddhist principles have special implications for social transformation. Nothing has any substantiality of its own, because everything is related to everything else and changes as they change. Impermanence means that no problem is intractable since it is part of larger processes that are constantly evolving, whether or not we notice. My generation grew up during a Cold War that would never end, until suddenly it did. Apartheid in South Africa seemed inflexible and implacable, but below the surface tectonic plates were gradually shifting and one day that political system collapsed. These characteristics are not always encouraging: things can slowly worsen too, and solutions as well as problems are impermanent. It depends on us to understand how things are changing and how to respond to those changes.

That highlights two other principles connected with impermanence and nonsubstantiality: non-dogmatism and *upaya*, "skillful means." Shakyamuni Buddha's own flexibility and Buddhism's lack of dependence upon any fixed ideology implies the pragmatism of praxis. We build whatever raft will work to ferry us to the other shore, and once there we don't carry it around on our backs. Nonattachment allows for the openness and receptivity which awaken *upaya:* imaginative solutions that leap outside the ruts our minds usually circle in.

Everything up to this point has been about means rather than ends: what Buddhism implies about *how* to engage rather than *what* to engage with. What should socially engaged Buddhists focus on? There are so many problems that we don't know where to start.

Whenever we try to address one, we soon realize that it is only one aspect of a larger set of issues. The absurdity of drug ads on television and in magazines ("Ask your doctor to prescribe…") is connected with other distortions introduced into medical practice by pharmaceutical companies, which in turn cannot be understood apart from the outrageous price of many medications, which contributes to the ridiculous cost of medical care, which is in large part a consequence of our disgraceful lack of a national health care system, which is certainly related to the lobbying power of insurance and pharmaceutical companies, which is one example of the more general problem of corporate influence on government, and so forth. Another obvious chain or constellation that comes to mind includes poor public transport, addiction to oil, global warming, weapon manufacturers, military aggression leading to more hatred and more terrorism, unprecedented federal deficits that affect all other funding, etc. A constellation that starts with consumerism could cover many pages.

All these relationships can be discouraging, insofar as they reinforce each other. However, not all linkages are equal and some factors are more important than others, which encourages us to look for the heart of the problem. The heart is a relatively small organ, but if it stops beating then what the rest of the body does makes no difference. To unpack the point of this analogy, I offer a cautionary tale from the mystic East.

I taught in a Japanese university for many years and, despite some fine colleagues, it taught me to loathe Japan's educational system. It's better described as an examination system, for that is the sole concern of the whole process. The main thing students learn from it is to hate studying, which mostly involves memorizing for multiple-choice questions; the exams do not usually include an essay, which means that students do not need to bother learning how to write, which also means that they do not learn how to think. By the time they get to university many of them are exhausted, if not functionally brain-dead, and university is generally accepted as a time to relax and enjoy oneself, rather than an opportunity to stretch and develop oneself in new ways. Academic standards are quite low and it is difficult to flunk out, because that would reflect back negatively on the university itself.

The consequences of this unfortunate system for many millions of bright young people, and for Japanese society as a whole, are tragic. Nevertheless, it would be easy to change. The focus is entirely on university entrance exams, and each university sets its own. There is also a strict hierarchy accepted by everyone: Tokyo University is the most prestigious, followed by Kyoto University, and so on in a recognized order. This means that if a dozen of the best universities reformed their admissions policies, other universities would soon feel compelled to follow their example, and Japan's whole educational system would re-structure to meet the new criteria. Why hasn't this happened? Despite a few gestures in that direction, the politicians and bureaucrats who supervise this system are more or less comfortable with it, and *juku* cram schools find it quite profitable. While some grumble, the basic problem with changing it is that most people now take it for granted.

The point of this story is the importance of locating the heart of a problem—which may be something we have learned to take for granted—and focusing on that. Is there something comparable for socially engaged Buddhists in the West to focus on? Is there a "black hole" at the core of the constellations mentioned above? I conclude with a reflection that also amounts to a suggestion.

Of course, the most important issue of all, and the context for all others, is ecological: global climate-change along with many less obvious human impacts on the biosphere that sustains us. We must do whatever we can, in alliance with others, but I suspect that Buddhism has little distinctive to offer in the short run, except for emphasizing less dualistic ways of thinking as an alternative to the worldviews that got us into this mess. We are now collectively at the point where everyone knows the direction we need to move in. The question is whether there is the political and economic will to do so.

Because of the widespread and palpable suffering it involves, and all its other deplorable repercussions, it is also essential that those of us living in the United States find ways to challenge American militarism in general and our Middle East foreign policy in particular. Since the political system has become so corrupt, perhaps the best place to direct our energies is military personnel themselves, to inform them about Buddhism and nonviolence, including non-cooperation with the war machine. We also need to challenge recruitment practices, especially in schools. Such programs would draw on our strength: education, reflection, perhaps instruction in meditation for those who ask for it. Members of the military—especially those in the lower ranks—already know a lot about the first noble truth. During the Vietnam War draft resistance and other forms of nonviolent but illegal protest played an important role in eventually ending the war. Similar actions may again become appropriate, or necessary.

Despite the importance of confronting militarism and ecological breakdown, however, I wonder if it would be better for socially engaged Buddhism to place top priority on something else, which would indirectly address those other two issues as well.

According to Buddhist teachings the solution to *dukkha* involves liberating one's awareness from the places it gets stuck. If the same is true socially—if our collective *dukkha* is due to our collective attachments—Buddhism may have a distinctive role to play in emphasizing the places where our collective awareness has become trapped, and showing how to liberate our awareness from those traps. To say it again, any such liberation calls for personal spiritual practice as well, but we also need to recognize and confront the institutionalized ways in which collective awareness traps have taken on a life of their own.

Perhaps the most influential example, and certainly the most pervasive, is advertising and public relations, which in the last century or so have evolved into a very sophisticated science of opinion- and desire-manipulation. Advertising is now so pervasive that we can hardly imagine a world without it. Yet several states—Hawaii, Alaska, Vermont, Maine, and Rhode Island—have banned new outdoor billboards, which helps to explain much of their beauty and attractiveness to tourists. Would our own minds become more beautiful and attractive without all the other forms of advertising that infect us from inside? Can we imagine a culture that did not accept the kinds of psychic manipulation now taken for granted? Alcohol and tobacco commercials are now strictly limited—why stop with them? A world in which most forms of advertising were reduced and restricted is no more unthinkable than prohibiting tobacco smoke in public places only a generation ago.

The difference is that excluding tobacco consumption from most public locations has a very small effect on the economy; addicts go outside to smoke. Severe curbs on advertising would have enormous repercussions for all of society, because consumerism depends upon it. That is why it *can't* be done (it would require restructuring the whole economy) and also why it *must* be done (if our consumption patterns are not natural but induced in such a fashion, the argument that they increase our happiness collapses). The Gross National Product could no longer be confused with our Gross National Happiness.

The fact that any such movement would be resisted tooth and nail points to the heart of the problem: the influence of major corporations, not only on the economy but also on the government and on our ways of thinking. U.S. militarism and foreign policy over the last century or so cannot be comprehended without noticing how they have served the interests of big American companies rather than the American people. Our public priorities make little sense (attacking Iraq? enormous military expenditures? no national health system? The growing gap between rich and poor? etc.) without understanding the role of corporate media in capturing our attention and molding our opinions. In a country that prides itself on its democratic traditions, they are the means by which self-serving elites have gained control over national priorities. They are probably the best (worst?) example of institutionalized *lack* that has assumed a life of its own, with goals (profit, stock price, market share) that can never be satisfied. The belief that those goals work to the benefit of everyone has been indoctrinated into the social fabric, as a truism that no reputable public figure is allowed to question. In reality, the future will be grim unless we can find ways to rein in corporate power.

Corporations are not mentioned in the U.S. Constitution and in the early years of the republic they were viewed warily and their activities restricted. They were incorporated only for the public good: what they could do and how long they could do it were limited. Toward the end of the nineteenth century, however, corporations (with a little help from corrupt legislatures and judges) began to rewrite the laws that control them, and today the power of major corporations has become truly formidable, of course. Nevertheless, they have an Achilles heel: the legal obligation to be chartered by governmental authorities makes them accessible to democratic control. The political and economic revolution that we most need, I suspect, is a mass movement to rewrite corporate charters, to subordinate them once again to the public good. Instead of companies being incorporated for an indefinite period, why not require the charters of large corporations to be renewed every decade or so? These could involve public hearings during which they must defend their activities. Companies that do not serve the public interest should be wound up and sold off. Every corporate board could also be required to have a labor representative and a publicly appointed member to evaluate the ecological consequences of major decisions.

These are only a few suggestions. They may be unfeasible, but in that case we must find alternative ways to subordinate the interests of incorporated institutions to the larger public good. If our present economic system cannot adapt to such priorities, we will need to develop a new one.

To sum up, what is distinctively Buddhist about socially engaged Buddhism? Emphasis on the social *dukkha* promoted by group-selves as well as by ego-selves, such as the three collective poisons of institutionalized greed, institutionalized ill will, and institutionalized delusion. The importance of personal spiritual practice, commitment to nonviolence, the flexibility implied by impermanence and non-substantiality, along with the realization that ending our own *dukkha* requires us to be concerned about the *dukkha* of everyone else as well. While we need to address the militarization of our society and the ecological impact of our economy, Buddhism has something more distinctive to offer with its implicit critique of the ways that our collective awareness has become trapped and manipulated. One place to start is by challenging the pervasive role of advertising, but in order to do that effectively I think that we will eventually find ourselves addressing the institutionalized social dukkha perpetrated and perpetuated by our globalizing, corporation-dominated economic system.

We may well feel overwhelmed by such a prospect, so in conclusion it is important to remember that any role socially engaged Buddhists might play will ultimately be minor, as part of a much larger movement for peace and social justice that has already begun to develop in the same direction. This movement has many faces and involves many different perspectives. However, Buddhist emphasis on the liberation of our collective attention suggests that a socially awakened Buddhism might have a distinctive role to play in clarifying what the basic problem really is.

Index

Acknowledgments

Earlier drafts of some of these chapters have appeared in *Tricycle, Shambhala Sun, Buddhadharma, Turning Wheel, Insight Journal,* and *Rightview Quarterly.* Somewhat different versions of "The Three Poisons, Institutionalized" appeared in *Mindful Politics* and *The Best Buddhist Writing 2007,* both edited by Melvin McLeod.

Special thanks to Josh Bartok for his excellent editing, as usual. It's always a pleasure to work with the people at Wisdom Publications, which this time included Rod Meade Sperry and Tony Lulek.

For their comments and encouragement, I am also grateful to Julian Bamford, Marcie Boucouvalas, Brendan Breen, Conrad Brunk, Lance Brunner, Ian Collins, Andrew Cooper, Harold Coward, John Crook, Tynettte Deveaux, Maia Duerr, David Gilner, Linda Goodhew, Ruben Habito, Ken Jones, Paul Knitter, David Levy, Kobutsu Malone, Melvin McLeod, Phra Paisal Visalo, Jordi Pigem, Leslie Rogers, Santikaro, Alan Senauke, James Shaheen, Mu Soeng, Jo Marie Thompson, Jonathan Watts, and many others whose names do not spring to mind right now.

About the Author

DAVID R. LOY is the Besl Professor of Ethics/Religion and Society at Xavier University and a Zen teacher in the lineage of Koun Yamada (author of *The Gateless Gate*). His other books include: *Nonduality: A Study in Comparative Philosophy, Lack and Transcendence: Death and Life in Psychotherapy, Existentialism and Buddhism, A Buddhist History of the West: Studies in Lack, The Great Awakening: A Buddhist Social Theory,* and *The Dharma of Dragons and Daemons: Buddhist Themes in Modern Fantasy* (with Linda Goodhew). He lives in Cincinnati with his wife Linda and son Mark.

About Wisdom Publications

Wisdom Publications, a nonprofit publisher, is dedicated to making available authentic works relating to Buddhism for the benefit of all. We publish books by ancient and modern masters in all traditions of Buddhism, translations of important texts, and original scholarship. Additionally, we offer books that explore East-West themes unfolding as traditional Buddhism encounters our modern culture in all its aspects. Our titles are published with the appreciation of Buddhism as a living philosophy, and with the special commitment to preserve and transmit important works from Buddhism's many traditions.

To learn more about Wisdom, or to browse books online, visit our website at www.wisdompubs.org.

You may request a copy of our catalog online or by writing to this address:

Wisdom Publications
199 Elm Street
Somerville, Massachusetts 02144 USA
Telephone: 617-776-7416
Fax: 617-776-7841
Email: info@wisdompubs.org
www.wisdompubs.org

The Wisdom Trust

As a nonprofit publisher, Wisdom is dedicated to the publication of Dharma books for the benefit of all sentient beings and dependent upon the kindness and generosity of sponsors in order to do so. If you would like to make a donation to Wisdom, you may do so through our website or our Somerville office. If you would like to help sponsor the publication of a book, please write or email us at the address above.

Thank you.

Wisdom is a nonprofit, charitable 501(c)(3) organization affiliated with the Foundation for the Preservation of the Mahayana Tradition (FPMT).

Also Available from Wisdom Publications

The Great Awakening
A Buddhist Social Theory
David R. Loy
320 pages, ISBN 0-86171-366-4, $16.95

"Now that I'm growing old, I look for deeper meaning everywhere. Loy's book sure gave me some—not only on that personal how-to-live-my-life level, but also in the universal realm of what's-this-all-about."—Kalle Lasn, Editor-in-Chief of *Adbusters*

Engaged Buddhism in the West
Edited by Christopher S. Queen
560 pages, ISBN 0-86171-159-9, $24.95

"A deep, rich, important offering that show hows engaged Buddhists are offering the fruits of their practice in very concrete ways in the West."
—Thich Nhat Hanh

Buddhist Peacework
Creating Cultures of Peace
Edited by David W. Chappell
256 pages, ISBN 0-86171-167-X, $14.95

"Thich Nhat Hanh, Stephanie Kaza, the Dalai Lama, and others offer new visions and methods that allow us to evaluate and strengthen our own understandings of nonviolence and the clearest ways to peace."—*FOR: The Fellowship of Reconciliation*

The New Social Face of Buddhism
A Call to Action
Ken Jones
Foreword by Kenneth Kraft
320 pages, ISBN 0-86171-365-6, $16.95

"A meticulous, philosophical foundation for compassionate social action and a clear explication of the social-action implications of Buddhist thought."
—*Publishers Weekly*

One City
A Declaration of Interdependence
Ethan Nichtern
224 pages, 0-86171-516-0, $15.95

"In a time when most Buddhist leaders seem up in the clouds and most political leaders seem lacking in moral imagination, Nichtern represents the wisdom of the in-between."—*The American Prospect*

Mindful Politics
A Buddhist Guide to Making the World a Better Place
Edited by Melvin McLeod
300 pages, ISBN 0-86171-298-6, $16.95

"The essays here gently push us to think beyond orthodox solutions, giving us inspiration and hope."—Howard Zinn